CW00433578

MARTIN ISRAEL

An Appreciation

Written and Compiled by

JOHN WYBORN

with additional material by

THE VERY REVD ALEX WEDDERSPOON

CFPSS

First Impression – 2013

ISBN 978-0-902666-47-4

Copyright CFPSS 2013

Published by
The Churches' Fellowship for Psychical and Spiritual Studies
The Rural Workshop, South Road, North Somercotes
Louth, Lincolnshire, LN11 7PT

Printed in Great Britain by
East Coast Grafix, North Somercotes, LN11 7LN

Contents

Introduction

This book has been prepared by friends and supporters of the Revd Dr Martin Israel to commemorate his life and work. Its publication has been timed to coincide with the Diamond Jubilee year of the Churches' Fellowship for Psychical and Spiritual Studies, of which Martin Israel was Chairman and later President over a number of years.

The material is presented in the following chapters or sections. First there is a biographical summary, taken partly from Martin Israel's own published works and amplified by reminiscences supplied by those who have written to us and who knew him at various stages of his life. Then we present a selection of extracts from the letters we have received. These illustrate Martin the man – the healing counsellor, spiritual director, priest and retreat conductor, psychic and mystic, complete with anecdotes illustrating many of his foibles and attitudes, which his friends will remember with amusement and affection.

Next follows a series of reflections upon some of the key spiritual writings of his, notably his earlier published books. Martin wrote spontaneously and inspirationally, much as he preached, introducing many different themes within a given subject. This makes the material very difficult to précis or summarise, especially as he himself was resistant to people trying to paraphrase or amend his language.

After this we present a brief summary of his other main published works. It is hoped that all of this material will stimulate an interest in his spirituality and faith, which in our opinion is more than ever relevant in the twenty-first century as it unfolds with all the social, political, religious and philosophical disputes and perplexities of today.

Then follows a chapter entitled, 'The Spiritual Wisdom of Martin Israel'. We are fortunate in having the Very Revd Alex Wedderspoon, Dean Emeritus of Guildford, as our President at this time, who has been able to cast a detached eye, as a senior churchman, over Martin Israel's published works. He has viewed them in the light of developments elsewhere in religious thought over the decades when Martin was writing and preaching. This was an onerous undertaking especially for one who had not known Martin Israel personally, and it involved some months of studying nearly all of Martin Israel's texts.

The result is a masterful summary of Martin's beliefs and teaching in the context of professional theology and inter-faith dialogue. He raises the interesting subject of why Martin Israel did not challenge or indeed refer in his writings to some of the more controversial religious issues of the day, some of which Alex describes. He suggests that this reticence might perhaps stem from Martin's initial perspectives within Judaism, or maybe due to his rapid preparation for Ordination, bypassing the full theological training, as one who was deemed not to need it, but which left him less equipped for religious debate than he might have been for a medical dispute of some kind. This is an interesting subject upon which to ponder. Some who knew him may also suggest that Martin Israel was 'simply not that sort of person'; that he was not interested in open controversy, especially not of the kind that might lead to his becoming what today might be called 'a celebrity'. He believed that he was divinely inspired and that he knew what he was doing. Was he also concerned, perhaps, that his rather special gifts of perception should not be dissipated through fame, fortune or public scrutiny?

To conclude, we append a section of acknowledgements in which we have attempted to list all those who have written to us or otherwise expressed support and encouragement for this book. This began with an approach to those on Martin Israel's Christmas card list, and it grew from there. Thanks are due to Bob Gilbert, Rosalind Smith and Julian Drewett of the Churches' Fellowship for valuable editorial and presentational support.

Martin Israel was an English mystic of the modern era, in the tradition of Dame Julian of Norwich and many others. We hope this book will re-awaken interest in his life and work, and lead to further study of his books in their original form.

1. A Biography

Martin Spencer Israel was born on 30 April 1927 to liberal Jewish parents in Johannesburg, South Africa, where his father was a respected eye surgeon From the age of three Martin became aware of a special calling or vocation that in time was to direct the purpose of his life, which became an unusual one. In his own words, recounted in the early pages of his book *Precarious Living*, 'I was not more than three when I heard, with the inward ear, a voice that addressed me directly in the darkness of my inner self, yet it carried with it a radiant light'. It offered him a preview of his future life. He was to pursue a lonely course, passing along a dark tunnel, as it were, alone and isolated. He would be shorn of the many reassurances of everyday life, and often misunderstood. He would be compelled to go on, even to his ultimate death in order to find the true purpose of his being. Yet even at that age he had a feeling that death was not the end, and that the humiliation of a difficult life lived honestly, were the necessary precursors of an ultimate glory. And it was a glory that embraced all people. In writing about those times he was aware of his precocity for a child of that age experiencing such things, yet he recalled that it did not bring him pleasure or happiness. It was a personal burden that he knew he had to bear, and yet not to betray the foreknowledge that had been given him.

He soon realised that his parents, much as he admired them, were not of a kind in whom he could confide his thoughts. They would have been embarrassed and uncomprehending, living as they did in the affluent, white-dominated South Africa of the inter-war years. An only child, there was no one in whom he could confide apart from the African servants employed at his home. It was through them that he felt able to identify true authenticity, rather than with the Europeans that he knew. In the African silences as well as in their joyful spontaneous singing he sensed a spiritual reality. These simple folk, who had little in the way of personal possessions, were able to demonstrate true love without the encumbrances of pride, covetousness or social pretensions. As a child Martin felt he could be most fully himself when he was with these people.

One day a servant girl, who could barely read or write, showed him an evangelical tract that she had been given. It told of a man who had cared sufficiently about the world to take on its full burden of sin and wickedness, to the extent of suffering a terrible death to bring about salvation. Martin then knew that it was He who had spoken to him. Moreover whatever he may agree or disagree with what was said about Him, he could never turn away from his life and his witness to the truth. From a Jewish upbringing Martin's work was to be one of reconciliation.

There was of course an immediate gauntlet to be run. At that age you had to behave in a way appropriate to a child. There were teachers who had to be respected whatever the depths of their understanding. And there were one's fellows who were generally far more concerned with success and dominance at games than with anything remotely spiritual. Parktown Boys School in Johannesburg, where Martin was a pupil, today displays on its website many of the worthy attributes of a traditional English boys' public school, with its emphasis on outgoing competitive team sports, and one imagines it was much the same in those days. But such places are not ideal development grounds for the introvert or the profound sensitive thinker. Martin records two negative outcomes from that period: a difficulty in asserting himself in the outer world, and a tendency to feel contempt for those who behave insensitively. He was inept at purely physical tasks and games – anyone who knew him in later life would feel dismay at even contemplating him being placed in a rugby football scrum. He was an easy target for the school bully. Martin surmounted these difficulties, though they left him with a sense of unreality in his relationships with other children. Much easier were the relationships he had with the African servants. Like many boys in a basically hostile school environment he took refuge in the mental side of his character. He usually managed to come top of his class, and that enabled him to survive with a modicum of self-respect, even rising above those who otherwise would have crushed him.

He adjudged himself a strange child. 'Silence I loved more than anything else!' he records. As a budding mystic he was even then aware of a communion with nature and the creation all around him. As he later observed, the true mystic is born not made. But at the same time there was a painful inability to communicate with his fellows, which later had to be overcome before the essence of mysticism could flourish.

Martin's first real contact with people as individuals came once again through African servants. There was a very obese woman who did the family washing each Monday. Martin hardly ever spoke to her, but he knew her and accepted her as part of the homestead. One week she did not appear, and on enquiry Martin was told simply that she had died of pneumonia during the week. Martin was stunned and began to appreciate the injustice of the society in which he lived. At the age of eight he met the coloured boyfriend of one of the maids. He was intelligent and mechanically adept but because of his colour he could get no commensurate work. He was also a heavy drinker, and once he came in wounded after a fight. Martin was struck by the contrast between his brown skin and the pink of his wounded chest wall. For the first time he began to think of medicine as a career. But the circumstances of the fight also impressed themselves upon him, especially when the man was later injured in another fight and died. By this time Martin was a convinced socialist, and although his political views changed later in life he never lost his concern for the underdog. Another concern of his was the evils of capital punishment, quite common at that time.

As he grew older he became an avid reader, preferring the classics to works of religion apart from the Bible. At the age of sixteen he prepared for the Matriculation examination. He was considered an outstanding pupil. This he recalls was primarily due to his attention to detail, and also the determination not to fail. If you can't play rugger you've got to succeed at something else and even coming second or third would be a disaster to the vulnerable scholar. It was on this occasion that he had a deep religious experience upon hearing Weber's Overture to 'Oberon', which he describes in *Precarious Living* and which involved becoming aware of all creation.

Upon leaving school he studied Medicine at Witwatersrand University where he was awarded a first class degree, in the course of which he grew further away from spiritual matters. But he could never forget what he had experienced. He was clumsy with his hands, which he ascribed to his earlier sheltered life where servants did all the work. This was ameliorated by working with patients and by dissection, though he never found relationships easy with other students. He could talk intellectually but never socially or with 'small talk', and he found it hard to show affection or make other contact. Asking for something in a shop was a major trial, whereas being invited to a party was something to be utterly dreaded. He ascribed this to his upbringing, describing his mother as possessive of her only child whereas his father's view of life was 'shallow and materialistic'. In fairness, however, he also acknowledged a gratitude for the beautiful home in which he was brought up. He was grateful for not having been packed off to a boarding school which might have subsumed him totally, and he recognised that some of his problems stemmed from a school system of those days that laid emphasis on discipline, exercise and conformity rather than a measure of individuality and intellect that might be allowed today.

Martin had to pass through a period of deep disillusionment where, despite his excellent academic qualifications, careers of lesser qualified people progressed ahead of his own due to his lack of social gifts. He found difficulty in obtaining house-doctor appointments.

In 1951 Martin Israel left South Africa for good and settled in England where he undertook postgraduate medical research, initially at Hammersmith Hospital in London. His parents accompanied him on a holiday to England before leaving him and saying farewell. He records the poignancy of parting from them for what would almost be the last time. He had a difficult relationship with his father, on account of what Martin described as his cynical view of the world. Martin records a feeling of actual hatred towards him as they said farewell, which he discovered later had to be faced and lived through, rather than denied, as part of a healing process. Martin then had to survive in a still relatively austere post-war London, with the remnants of food rationing until 1954. Also he had all of the social handicaps that accompanied him as part of the baggage of his upbringing. He sometimes lived alone in a bed-sit and sometimes in the hospital mess, preferring the latter since he at least was in the company of others even though he could not easily communicate.

In due course Martin had to serve two years National Service in the Royal Army Medical Corps, which he found far less exacting than he had feared. As a qualified doctor he was awarded a commission. Much of his time was spent in Nigeria and Cyprus, where he felt he learned a lot, though still with his social disadvantages. His later friend and colleague Dr Robert Jones reckons he was unlucky in being conscripted at all at the age of 26, since the obligation ended at that age. But Martin was not one to shirk his duty. In Cyprus he encountered the man who was to be the future Head of the Department of Pathology at the Royal College of Surgeons (RCS).

After National Service the return to civilian life brought once again its problems. Shorn of organised group activities, there was the need to pursue a meaningful existence despite all the social disabilities. 'I had to face my dereliction', he records, 'and ask myself what life was really all about, and what I hoped to achieve'. By this time Martin had become a university lecturer, and he was becoming aware that his social inhibitions were going to be a bar to his academic progress. The spiritual darkness of his teenage years descended once again, and there was a dread which he found hard to define. Prayer, which had been his mainstay, became of little value. He longed to be safe and home, but there was no home. He tried desperately to be sociable to those around him; to speak enthusiastically about 'nothing in particular'. But the mastery of polite small talk was never to be within his grasp, as those will testify who knew him much later in his life. He records that he was experiencing 'the dark night of the soul'. He felt that all he managed to achieve was an attempt to propagate scandal in an endeavour to appear witty and sophisticated. When he perceived what he was doing he felt ashamed, and so withdrew further into his shell. In retrospect he reflected that others were probably also going through these trials in self-development, despite outwardly showing confidence.

Matters came to a head when, having to speak in a large lecture theatre, he found he could not raise his voice. He sought help from an accomplished speech therapist, who at once diagnosed muscle spasm brought on by tension, fear and anxiety. Treatment involved relaxation and voice projection with breathing exercises, which within a remarkably short time enabled him to speak loudly and clearly. He was fortunate in that his therapist had herself suffered from speech difficulties, and urged Martin also to seek psychiatric or psychological help. This he was initially reluctant to do, being prejudiced at that time against the atheistic and anti-religionist stance of many Freudian practitioners. Later a neighbour introduced him to a London County Council course being run on psychology, held at the Iona Education Centre in South Kensington. Expecting a highly qualified professor of psychiatrics, he actually found a large, elderly woman named Mary Macaulay who had no qualifications but a great deal of experience. A Scottish Presbyterian who had lived in Canada, her outlook was universalist and she was not a churchgoer. She knew her subject, however, and knew enough about Freud, Adler and Jung – especially Jung – to provide the counselling and understanding that was needed. The title of her course, 'Understanding Ourselves', arguably spoke for itself. She emphasised the spiritual nature of the human being, and was sympathetic to the notion of reincarnation. Martin became friendly with others attending the course, and at last began to find people with whom he could converse freely. His loneliness lessened. He began to assist Mary Macaulay by speaking at the Centre, and it was here that he discovered that he had the gift of spontaneous inspirational speech without notes. This made him much in demand as a lecturer, as his own views were also universalist, and in due course this led to his development as a retreat conductor, and later to ordination.

Martin had now found a way through many of his difficulties. He emerged reassured that there was nothing deeply or seriously wrong with him. He was just an unusual person, but there was nothing wrong in that. This knowledge enabled him to come to himself, and released him from many of his previous inhibitions. Inevitably there are difficulties which arise in these circumstances, and he recalled that in a fit of aggression he wrote a series of very unpleasant letters to his father, which, however, he describes as being 'distinctly pertinent'. It took seven years to reach a reconciliation which he felt was necessary for the healing of his own soul, apart from which he was able to channel any aggressive instincts into more progressive channels.

Martin Israel was a very private person, and it may be felt that his relations with his parents are not of direct concern to the twenty-first century reader. This is, however, a book about his life and work. His capacity and gifts as a counsellor are thus within our remit, including how he may have acquired them and aspects of his life that may have made him what he was should therefore perhaps be touched upon, no matter how sensitive. Towards the end of his life he produced a final work *Everlasting Goal* which was published privately. In this, he writes of his parents: 'My mother was quarrelsome and neurotic, and my father was a paedophile who practised fulsomely on me. My mother's nature ensured that I would have no friends, while my father's assault on my body degraded me so that I always felt inferior to my classmates at school. I have therefore had an inferiority complex. It was in this background that I experienced God as a natural gift, for my family, though Jewish, had little time for worship. My parents attended synagogue for a time, but found it ultimately of little use to them, and became indifferent to their native religion'. But later in the same book he adds: 'I have through the grace of God forgiven my parents and remember them with affection. They obviously came to me for a purpose to make me what I am; I can now thank them for the care they bestowed upon me. I have moved in a direction they could not have anticipated. But I do not believe events occur fortuitously. At any rate they did not stand in my way'.

To the extent that these sentences represent Martin Israel's final recollections of his home life, we have perhaps an indication of the extent to which he was so effective as a counsellor and healer. In many respects he was the archetype 'wounded surgeon' of T. S. Eliot's 'East Coker':

'The wounded surgeon plies the steel,
That questions the distempered part.
Beneath the bleeding hands we feel

The sharp compassion of the healer's art'

or as Jung put it 'a good half of every treatment that probes at all deeply, consists of the doctor's examining himself'. The subject of paedophilia is an emotive one that, in a lifetime, has sprung from an extreme state of a community-in-denial to one of hatred and persecution of the offender that at times borders upon a witch-hunt. Hideous as is this intimate physical assault of the powerful upon the weak, one feels that Martin himself would be concerned to seek, to treat and to cure the underlying causes, be they physical or psychological or, as some would have it, just plain sin – some of it inherited.

Dr Susan Heyner, who knew him during that period, records 'I was a research fellow in the Department of Anatomy at the RCS from 1961 to 1963. During that time I became friends with Martin Israel. I forget how we met initially, but we connected on several levels. We published a short communication together dealing with the examination of roller tube tissue cultures using the electron microscope. But we were kindred spirits in that we both loved classical music. Martin and I went to a number of concerts together. We were also interested in spirituality and had discussions on this topic and exchanged books. Martin was extremely shy. In 1963 I married and left London to come to the USA. At that time Martin asked if he could buy my music system, as though he wanted something to remember me by. He was a very dear individual and I was happy to learn about his subsequent career'.

Following this period of self-discovery, Martin discovered he had two gifts. The first of these was an ability to reach at will what he described as formless contemplation, a gift which many people strive to achieve in a lifetime. This released in him psychic gifts he previously feared he had lost. He could sense other people's dispositions and needs, as well as sensing the presence of evil. He found that when silent and still he could sometimes sense communication from friends who had died, and who now existed in a wider sphere.

The second gift, for which he later became celebrated among those who knew him, was an ability to speak on spiritual matters spontaneously and inspirationally. This he could do for up to an hour with no notes or script in a manner that suggested divine inspiration. The ability to do this was, he felt, bound up with the suffering and experience he had had, as well as his intellectual knowledge, and this enabled him to practise the gift without the kind of self-aggrandisement that many people would have felt and which would undoubtedly have caused the gift to abate.

Martin reckoned that it took him a further five years from the time of the restoration of his spiritual awareness before he was ready to undertake what became his real ministry. While he was gaining confidence socially and also developing contemplative prayer, his professional life was beginning to flourish. His proficiency as a teacher and lecturer also flourished following his speech therapy, and he was by this time a lecturer in pathology at the RCS. However, 'It was unfortunate that at this time internecine strife broke out at the place where I worked', he recounts.

Dr Robert Jones, a colleague of his at the Royal College in those days, writes as follows:

'Martin and I met in September 1959 in the department of pathology at the RCS, when I took up an appointment as research assistant funded by the British Empire Research Campaign. He had been appointed the previous year as one of the three lecturers in the department. Together with the professor, they gave lectures to postgraduate doctors studying for the Fellowship of the RCS, an essential step in a surgeon's career.

One of the striking things about Martin was that his appearance changed hardly at all over the five or so decades during which I knew him. He was naturally shy and retiring and gave the impression of nervousness. I never heard him laugh outright; instead he expressed amusement as a kind of high-pitched buzzing chuckle, rocking backwards and forwards with his hands over his knees if he happened to be sitting down. Although he appreciated humour, not once can I ever recall him telling a joke. Sometimes he permitted himself amusing and perceptive remarks about colleagues, but only when they were thoroughly deserved. I never knew him to be unkind.

Over the long period of our friendship Martin said very little about himself. Now and again a chance remark would reveal a sparse detail about his life. For a while he was associated with the medical school at the University of Witwatersrand though I did not know the exact nature of his position. He mentioned that it was forbidden to give anatomy tuition to black students. The reason may have been, as my poor memory allows, that some of the cadavers were those of white women. Martin saw the restriction for the apartheid nonsense that it was, and took the risk of conducting clandestine classes for African students. Although he did not speak of any professional risk, in those oppressive days his behaviour might well have meant instant dismissal.

It would be neither inaccurate nor unfair to write that the department of pathology was a singularly unhappy one. Certain members of staff were instructed to spy on the rest of us and to report anything untoward back to the professor. We knew that a woman research fellow, the senior technician, two successive secretaries and one of the cleaning staff were members of this select group. On two occasions I was carpeted for misdemeanours which I did not commit.'

Dr Jones describes how, in playful mood, he devised a game of snakes and ladders to illustrate the departmental politics. To climb a ladder one had to do something sycophantic, like digging the professor's garden. But to do something useful like writing a book, making a discovery, publishing a paper, or anything else that might further one's career, would result in your sliding down a snake. There were many more snakes on the board than there were ladders. Despite these unpleasant undercurrents, Martin was sufficiently senior to keep out of trouble.

Dr Jones continues, 'At one time one of the lecturers was being savagely and unfairly victimised by the professor to the point of dismissal, an event in which the woman researcher played a central role. Martin did what he could to help the man'. He describes evidence that anyone who applied for other positions were 'badmouthed' by the professor behind their backs. Only the woman spy and another lecturer enjoyed the professor's support.

Dr Jones then relates how in 1961, probably to cause the lecturers annoyance, the professor suddenly instructed that the topics taught to the students were to be changed. This added significantly to their teaching burden. 'Together with his colleague John Walter', he records, 'Martin put the imposition to advantage. On the quiet they planned and wrote a textbook of pathology. The professor was beside himself with anger when he discovered what they had been up to and managed to delay publication. Despite his unwillingness he was compelled by the Dean of the Institute of Biomedical Science (IBMS) to write a favourable foreword. Martin told me with great glee how each new development had thwarted the professor.

'The first edition of *General Pathology* by Walter and Israel was published in 1963 but the professor was not done. Although the book was tailor-made to fit the teaching course for the Fellowship examination, the title was initially kept off the recommended reading list. It was an instant runaway success, and netted considerable royalties. Years later, when the next edition came out, I remember seeing in the university bookshop, HK Lewis, tall piles of scruffy, well-thumbed second-hand copies of the first edition standing forlornly unsold on the floor. After John Walter, unable to find another post in the United Kingdom, moved to Canada, Martin took over the book himself. In all there were six editions, the last appearing in 1987.'

Dr Jones remembers that although Martin's position in the College was more secure than his own, their positions were tenuous and they would joke about it. 'Into the street!', they would murmur, as they passed one another in the corridor. But it was no joking matter.

Dr Jones relates how one summer evening in 1963 the doorbell rang at their Marylebone flat and there, unexpectedly, was Martin. He had attended a Harley Street reception organised by the dean, had felt out of place, and had decided to pay them a call rather than return to his lodgings. He and his wife were delighted to see him and they spent a pleasant hour together. The incident illustrated Martin's loneliness and isolation, even from his peers.

He then relates how Martin Israel was not really happy in Pathology and would have liked to move on. In competition with each other, they both applied for the Lilian May Coleman Fellowship in Cancer Research in late 1966. Dr Jones secured the post and Martin generously congratulated him afterwards. "I always felt it was not really for me", Martin admitted. "At heart I am not a research man". Martin did not socialise within the College. He had no close friends there, though he was well respected. The pathology book enhanced his status considerably. In 1969 he assisted Dr Jones in a study into the carcinogenic effects of CS gas which, as it happened, produced no specific results.

'By that time all was not well in the IBMS', Dr Jones recalls. 'In the 1960s students were drawn from all parts of the Commonwealth especially Australia. The fees provided vital income for the College but after these countries began to set up their own examination boards students' numbers began to fall off. The Institute fell victim to falling income. In the late 1970s its departments were dismantled one by one. Many of the staff were able to retire.'

But by this time Martin's life and work had taken other directions.

Martin Israel himself comments upon those years, during which he realised that professional advancement was out of the question. He felt that he learned that an effective spiritual perspective, far from making one less fit for the cut and thrust of practical life, in fact provides strength. Though tempted to move on, he was sustained by a sense of vocation to stay where he was and to pursue his immediate calling. He perceived that, as he put it, only by suffering does one become proficient in life and able to love others.

At about this time he had a prophetic dream. He was walking down a street and fell into an open manhole. He found himself in a cavern with many passages, opening into rooms where people were pursuing drab occupations, until passing through he came to an operating theatre. There it was made plain to him that, having learnt all that he could be taught about healing the body, he should now return to the world where, although the sun was only shining dimly, there was a hope of some promise if he were to progress.

The path he knew he had to follow was one to a knowledge of God, The people he now began to associate with were themselves following a similar path, though not all of them would have acknowledged it in so many words. Raised initially in the liberal Jewish faith, he greatly valued

Judaism. He never experienced anti-Semitic prejudice and never once considered changing his name as some Jewish people did. Yet Christ had been revealed to him in childhood. He came to believe that God was thus greater than the Jewish religion and that Christ was there universally for all people. Logically he might have converted as soon as he was beyond his parents' influence, but this was not so. Whilst recognising that religion included saintly people of all kinds, many of the early Christians he met both in South Africa and elsewhere were far from divinely inspired. He found them selfish, mean, racial, and as dishonest as many who professed no faith at all. Arguably they were worse because they displayed additionally a kind of sanctimony he found even less attractive. Mystical awareness, he discovered, was rare in both Judaism and Christianity.

Upon reaching England Martin separated himself from Judaism and for a while remained unattached to any creed. The religious atmosphere of the nineteen-fifties he found self-assured and triumphalistic. The breakthrough for him came with the coming of Pope John XXIII, humanising what had previously been the most reactionary of all the Christian churches, and with Pierre Teilhard de Chardin, the mystic. Radical re-thinking was in the air. For a while he joined a non-credal group of Christians who did not believe in the divinity of Christ and ignored most of the miracles in the New Testament. Though finding this teaching inadequate after a while, he found his fellows refreshingly honest in their profession. He evaluated various movements of that period; the 'New Age' the 'Age of Aquarius', and the Charismatic Renewal. Spiritualism he examined and discarded, being concerned at the level of reliance that mediums and other practitioners placed upon spirit guides, who may or may not be sound.

Finding himself involved with the Ministry of Healing, he was initially cautious. Experience in scientific medicine had made him professionally unsure of a process that was not amenable to reason. It was at the behest of a very skilled psychic healer that he was persuaded himself to practise the laying on of hands, which to begin with he did rather ashamedly, taking care never to accept reward of any kind or payment – a policy which he subsequently always adhered to. Martin recalled the bigoted attitude of some religionists of that period, who would claim religious healing if it occurred within their orbit as valid, whereas anything outside orthodoxy as they perceived it was automatically the work of the devil. Martin studied Jung, Maslow and other psychological thinkers. He assessed and appreciated all the main Christian churches: the Catholics for their liturgy, the Protestants for the priesthood of the individual believer, and the Quakers for their consistency over time.

Between 1966 and 1972 he delivered a series of addresses at conferences held by the Seekers Trust, in Addington Park, Kent, and for a while he served as their President. The Trust had been founded in the 1920s by Charles Simpson who discovered he had healing gifts. Over the years many people had benefited from this and an estate had been acquired near West Malling where members could live and hold seminars and healing prayer circles. Two notable residents of the Seekers Trust were Frances Banks and Helen Greaves, whose book *Testimony of Light* gave comfort to so many.

At about that period he was also a frequent speaker at the Westminster Pastoral Foundation, nowadays known as WPF, which began its existence at the Methodist Central Hall, Westminster. It was through the vision, effort and persistence of the Methodist Minister Dr William Kyle that the charity came into being in 1969. William Kyle, with his wife Benita, recognised how psychological therapy - and in particular the insights and skills of the psychodynamic and psychoanalytic traditions - could transform pastoral support work with communities. Sadly Dr Kyle died in 1980 but his wife Benita recalls their friendship with Martin Israel. 'My husband was a practical man', she recounts, 'having trained as an engineer. Martin was quite the opposite, and useless at any kind of manual work, so their friendship offered valuable compensations'. The Kyles had at that time a holiday home in Robertsbridge where Martin would visit. Later he bought a cottage there himself which they helped him furnish, and which he enjoyed for many years into the 1980s. He spoke at Dr Kyle's funeral, which was a great comfort to his widow.

Martin had by that time begun to establish himself as a retreat conductor and a minister of healing, so that one of his clients, an Anglican priest, urged him to become a priest also. He suspected that Martin had not been baptised although receiving Holy Communion during many of the retreats, which was not strictly allowed. A hasty baptism and confirmation was performed on one evening so that Martin's Christian allegiance was established. By that time his devotion to Christ and the level of his religious knowledge was so obviously established through his retreat work that the diocesan bishop arranged that he be excused attendance at a theological college. He was instead given a course of instruction by Dr Eric Abbott, then Dean of Westminster, a staunch friend and supporter and who was delighted that he was to be ordained. Some of his friends from the Iona Education Centre were distressed at this decision, thinking that it would constrain his universalistic stance, but Martin had no doubts. After being made a deacon on 22 December 1974, he was admitted to the priesthood at St Paul's Cathedral on 21 September 1975. He was attached as unpaid curate to St Michael's Church, Cornhill, in the City of London for three years.

The late Sylvia Button recorded the following account of the ordination, taken from a letter of the time written by Vera Staff:

'You will have heard of Martin Israel's Ordination at St Michael's, Cornhill. The church usually has a congregation of about a dozen, but on that Sunday it was full to the doors. There were three Bishops, one Archdeacon, and both the present and the recently retired Deans of Westminster, with psychiatrists, marriage guidance counsellors, Samaritans, and I don't know who else in the congregation. The ceremonies were at once impressive and simple. Martin was just himself, looking a little solemn, like a grown up choirboy (he was the only ordinand), shy and thoughtful. When the Bishop of London, Dr Ellison, took his hand and led him down the chancel, he looked absolutely radiant. Thinking of the Church as a family, it was just like a family occasion, natural and not at all pompous. Atmosphere perfectly lovely.' Sylvia Button also records that Martin's reception into the Church had taken place on Easter Eve 1971, and that he had preached at a three-hour Good Friday Convent Service in 1972.

It was said that the existing incumbent was a little startled to find all manner of folk approaching his newly ordained assistant for deep spiritual counsel. In 1983 Bishop Graham Leonard, by this time Bishop of London, encouraged him to take the parish of Holy Trinity, Prince Consort Road, in South Kensington, first as Curate and then as Priest-in-Charge. The understanding was that he would be free to continue his work as a retreat conductor for some 15-20 engagements each year, as well as to fulfil a number of other counselling commitments in the ministry of healing which he regarded as an essential part of his work. He officially retired from the RCS in 1982.

The large Kensington parish which Martin took over was said to have fallen upon hard times, but in his period of office it soon began to recover. Situated next to the Royal College of Music and near the Royal Albert Hall, there became established a small but devoted choir of dedicated singers ensuring a high standard of music each Sunday. Martin Israel was an upholder of traditional liturgy, and visitors would expect Book of Common Prayer Matins or Holy Communion, with readings from the King James Bible. These were becoming harder to find in other churches. Above all there were his inspirational sermons delivered spontaneously from the pulpit which in time brought, if not a huge congregation, a committed and wholly dedicated one emanating from far outside Kensington, as well as a devoted local following. Martin did not attract "the great and the good". Nor did he believe in overt evangelism, considering the correct way to propagate the faith was by example. Those who came tended more to be "the halt and the lame" who had their own desperate needs that Martin alone was able to meet.

Barbara Brooks, his parish secretary between 1986 and 1988 recalls: 'Martin loved classical music, so that the high quality of the choral music at Holy Trinity must have been a joy to him. He was ably supported by Major Jervis Gubbins, a longstanding churchwarden until his death in 1987, who took on the administration of the church very ably. This must have greatly relieved Martin. Major Gubbins would write detailed notes on all matters to do with the Parochial Church

Council, and Martin came to rely upon him for checking draft minutes and suchlike. Martin was always courteous and grateful for the little things that people did for him and he made a point of thanking them. This encouraged them to help the more. We all knew that he was special and that his post at Holy Trinity was only part of his work.

Martin had his first episode of what was diagnosed later as epilepsy in 1984. It caused dislocation of his left shoulder. In hospital he told me he had fought with "the angel of death", and additional surgery was performed at that time. When I saw him there he was sitting in a chair by his bed. Having read his cards and letters from well-wishers he laid them out separately on the bed so that it was almost completely covered. It seemed to show an appreciation of the love and care which people had sent to him and which he was allowing to flow from the pages. About a month after his return we were dismayed to see his other arm in a sling. The same thing had happened. Then followed the diagnosis of epilepsy and in due course medication was prescribed. Meanwhile I remember hearing his shoulder clicking as he celebrated Holy Communion. He bore the dislocations very bravely and I never heard him complain, although he must have been going through a bewildering and very painful period. After the surgery I do not think his shoulders ever fully recovered. He appeared to be left with a limitation of movement and he obviously found shaking hands with people difficult because he couldn't extent his arm in the usual way.'

As previously stated, Holy Trinity Church was not high-profile or "fashionable" in Martin's time, and he was openly uneasy with some of the latest popular trends in Anglican worship at that time. His incumbency continued until 1996 when a slow decline in his health, brought on by the onset of Parkinsonism as well as the epilepsy, made it necessary for him to retire. Sadly the termination was not pleasant. It became apparent that he could not continue, and he had turned 70 years of age when clergy normally retire. Accordingly the Church authorities decided that the incumbency should be terminated forthwith, and it all happened quite suddenly. Inevitably Martin found this 'nasty, brutish and short' and though he later became reconciled to it, the manner of his going might well have contributed to a sudden further critical decline in his health. After his eventual recovery he never quite felt the same about the church. 'This room is my church', he would say of the place where he lived and received visitors, and there was always a Bible and a prayer book on the table. His parishioners in South Kensington, however, were devastated. One Sunday he was there; the next week he had left them forever. Tears were shed in the shattered congregation on the following Sunday, when he failed to appear and the parishioners knew that they had lost a priest whom they could never replace.

However due to the dedication of his faithful friend and parish secretary through those years, Jennifer Howard, and to some other devoted followers, records of the spontaneous sermons were preserved on cassette and some of them were later reproduced. Together with Martin's short but inspirational messages in the monthly parish magazines, selections were printed by the Churches' Fellowship for Psychical and Spiritual Studies in booklet form which are still available today. For the most part they have stood the test of time and are as relevant now as they were then.

During the period of the 1970s through the 80s and 90s, Martin became closely involved in the work of two notable organisations that promoted spirituality. One of these was the Churches' Fellowship for Psychical and Spiritual Studies. He was elected Chairman in 1975, having previously been Vice-Chairman. The President was the Revd Dr Garth Moore, Chancellor of the Diocese of Southwark, whom Martin succeeded as President in 1983 remaining in that office until his resignation in 1998. The Churches' Fellowship had originally been founded in 1953 by a retired army officer, Lt-Col Reginald Lester, with the support of a number of the clergy at that time, and after discussion with Air Chief Marshal Lord Dowding, the former Head of Fighter Command in the Battle of Britain. Lord Dowding's concern with the paranormal and with the well-being of airmen who had been killed in the War, was well-known. Col Lester, a veteran of World War I, had been put off all religion by the horrors of that conflict. Having lost his wife suddenly on Christmas Day at the end of World War II, he was resolved to find out more about life after death. The result of this was an inter-denominational Christian organisation that, at its height in the early 1960s, had grown to some five thousand members. A great many clergy as well as lay people joined, with local groups all round the country. They conducted studies into aspects of the paranormal and were also concerned with the ministry of healing.

At the time of Martin's involvement many of these groups had evolved into what was later described as a kind of pseudo-spiritualism. Members frequently conducted séances, to the extent that both Martin Israel and Garth Moore felt that they had become incompatible with sound Christian principles and true spirituality. Barbara Bunce, in her history of the Fellowship entitled *So Many Witnesses*, records also the difficulties that there had been in reconciling modern scientific medicine with the churches' ministry of healing, made less easy by the apparent situation that many gifted mediums also demonstrated healing gifts. She describes this whole area as 'the greatest minefield' that they had had to face, and had actually dated from the 1950s when Dorothy Kerin, founder of Burrswood, was a Fellowship member. To help clarify the matter Chancellor Garth Moore stated in 1977, 'the Christian believes in the Communion of Saints, which means the communion of all Christians, living and departed. All we know is that when healing is effected the only true healer is God', though at the time not everyone agreed with this statement as it stood. Martin himself recorded in *The Pain that Heals* that he had no doubt that it is God's will that all creatures should be healed, but that God's healing is of a different order from that which mankind tends to envisage. We look for outward signs, relief and recovery. God looks for a transfigured person.

Martin Israel's early work with the President, which cannot have been easy, involved disciplining and shutting down a number of groups whose practice was felt to be incompatible with the teachings of the church. This task would not have been to Martin's taste, but those who knew him will recall that he could on occasion be sharp and decisive when he felt that the need arose. Ultimately the result was the continuance of the Fellowship as an organisation that, albeit smaller, could continue to justify acceptance and respect in established mainstream church circles.

The other organisation, of which Martin was President from 1983 to 1990, was the Guild of Health. The Guild had been founded many years previously by the Revd Jim Wilson, whose brother Edward had been greatly respected as a member of Captain Scott's ill-fated expedition to Antarctica, in which he had lost his life. Jim Wilson was an exponent and practitioner of contemplative meditation. As well as it being an accepted spiritual exercise in itself, Jim Wilson promoted the idea that a truly well-oriented soul by meditation could promote health in themselves and in others, and he became celebrated in the field of Christian spiritual healing, especially during the post-war years of the 1950s. Based in Edward Wilson House, a building just off Harley Street named in memory of the deceased explorer, the Guild flourished over that period with healing groups that would pray for those with severe illness. Jim Wilson himself would preach at parishes around the country on the value of meditation.

The Revd Dr Denis Duncan, who succeeded Martin as President of the Guild of Health, writes:

'I first encountered Martin Israel when I was part of his Meditation Group which met for some years at the Westminster Pastoral Foundation where I was Associate Director and Training Supervisor. We then met on various conferences where we both had speaking responsibilities, and I was familiar with his extempore talks and lectures. The particular connection I remember with some modest pride is the part I played in creating his remarkable writing ministry. It all began because I said to the then religious director of Hodder & Stoughton, "If I were you I would sign up Martin Israel on a ten year contract." Martin was invited to lunch, but the director said afterwards that he had no idea what Martin was talking about. Fortunately his company chairman was also present who said "sign him". The result was his first book *Summons to Life*'. This was to be followed by many others.

That episode illustrates how key decisions may hang on a thread. The many books that Martin Israel later wrote and published contributed substantially to his reputation. Today those who may not have heard of him in any other context, especially among the clergy, will respond when his name is mentioned, 'Yes indeed. I've read his books'.

Martin's work as a retreat conductor was such that one had to book months ahead to get a place on one of them. As always he spoke inspirationally without notes, and laid great stress upon silence. He had a measure of mental telepathy with those present, and many people reported that, as it were out of the blue, he would deal with some subject that was troubling them even though not directly part of the subject matter of the talk.

This work and his parish work continued until 1996 when Martin's consciousness began to show peculiar lapses and his walking, never very good, became more and more defective. A tremor also developed, and all this was correctly diagnosed as the beginnings of Parkinson's disease. Unfortunately it was not fully controlled and began to make his parish work impossible, leading to his retirement. His right knee became painful and two operations were performed. His general health continued to deteriorate until June 1997 when his consciousness deteriorated further. He was not himself and there was severe amnesia. He became barely able to walk and communication was restricted to 'yes' and 'no'. He seemed to suffer a complete systemic breakdown and even eating became a problem. From semi-consciousness he finally became totally unconscious and was admitted to hospital. During this time he seemed to descend into a vast pit of darkness in which he could sense the souls of a vast group of people quite unknown to him. It was as if he was in hell, and he afterwards commented that it might even have been literally so.

During this period friends visited him. He received the Eucharist and was anointed more than once. He had no recollection of any of this, and apparently lay in the balance between life and death, though he had no recollection of any fear.

Then one morning in July 1997 he attained normal consciousness. It felt like waking up after a night's sleep, he said, and the sun was shining. The ward sister told him, apparently with some amusement, that he had been fully unconscious for five weeks. He was remarkably well adjusted, though he suffered from amnesia as regards recent events, and could not walk. It took him more than six months with physiotherapy to learn to walk again. Total convalescence took longer, and he used a wheelchair for the rest of his life. Although it was known that he had epilepsy, he asked his hospital neurologist what really was the cause of this episode of collapse. The consultant admitted that nobody knew for certain, but it was apparent that he improved under a drug called levodopa in adequate quantities. Levodopa is a drug commonly used to treat Parkinsonism.

Martin Israel was at pains to examine the nature of what had happened to him. Was it physical or was it psychical – a near-death experience? He found himself more outspoken than before, but less impatient. He had a greater self-confidence and believed himself to be a 'nicer' person. He recorded that he no longer had any fear of death, and that were he to be told he would die that day he would have no concern. But what was the nature of his apparent descent into hell? He was never sure, accepting that at times of physical stress the brain may receive anomalous or inconclusive information.

After the death of his parents, Martin had no close living relatives. Left to himself the steady decline in his health over the final two decades of his life could have left him deeply vulnerable. Fortunately he had one family that befriended and supported him over those years. Marina, the Viscountess Cowdray, recalls, 'Martin was my grandmother's great friend and during a difficult period in his life, when he spoke about having a battle with an evil spirit, he asked my grandmother if he could stay with her during this period. She was struck by him and being an open-minded lady, she was rivetted by his story and spoke to us very openly about this spirit that fought with him in the pulpit. He became a close family friend and married Michael and myself and christened all our five children. It was my good fortune that I had Martin in my life as, similarly to Martin himself, I had an encounter with an evil spirit in 1994. During this period Martin helped me through this and managed to take away this spirit. So I grew to understand his work on a deeper level. It was around this time that I was asked to be his next of kin and look after all his financial affairs. Michael and I took on this role, and Rupert my brother took on the caring role for Martin for the last ten years of his life.

Martin's bust was given to me on his death and I have put it up in his honour in the Cowdray Chapel. Like a guardian angel that he was, I know he looks after all the meditators that spend time in the chapel. Martin believed in the power of prayer and meditation; and he was most content when sitting in silence. I have come to understand his awkwardness as it is through silence that all is revealed. Everything came to him through this method and he operated his life through prayer. There was in fact nothing to say. He was disappointed with the Church and felt liberated when he was away from the Church. It stifled him and he saw its limitations. He did not feel that he had been well treated by the Church but he was not a man to carry any judgement. He spoke often of his work on the other side with a lady. It was through her that a lot of his healing was conducted.'

The bust of Martin Israel is understood to be one of several sculptures of him by the celebrated sculptress Josefina de Pasconcellos, whose deep friendship with Martin began in the 1980s and is mentioned in the biography of her by Margaret Lewis. Among Josefina's many works she is known for her bronze of 'Reconciliation' mounted in the ruins of the old Coventry Cathedral, which was sponsored by Richard Branson.

For some years Martin Israel had occupied a large roomy first floor flat in Tregunter Road, South Kensington. Visitors to him there will recall the breakneck flight of stairs that approached the entrance door, with a dangerous twist near the top. Following the breakdown in his health there was no question of him continuing to live there. Fortunately the royalties from the book on pathology as well as his lecturer's pension, together with any family inheritance and the attentions of an erudite stockbroker, had ensured that he was not a poor man. Marina Cowdray's brother Rupert, who was experienced in the property world, was able to arrange the conversion of a Victorian house in Soudan Road, close to Battersea Park, and which backed on to his own property in the next street. He was able to install Martin there, after his discharge from hospital, supported by two able carers from New Zealand. One of these, Cliff, together with his wife Georgie, remained with Martin to the end of his life, devotedly taking him everywhere he needed to go. Martin by this time was finding the English winters trying, and they often spent the winter months either in New Zealand or, later, in Barbados which Martin especially liked.

Martin lived in Soudan Road quietly over the years from 1997, in steadily declining health but not unhappily, until his death on 23 October 2007, at the age of 80 after a short period in the Chelsea and Westminster Hospital. Friends visited him over that period of ten years, and he wrote two books one of which, *Everlasting Goal,* was published privately in 2005 by his friends Rupert, Cliff and Georgie, and dedicated to Anthea, a special confidante of his. There was a full congregation of his loving friends and supporters at his funeral service on Monday 5 November 2007 in Holy Trinity Church, Prince Consort Road, where he had been Honorary Curate from 1977 to 1982 and Priest-in-Charge between 1983 and 1996. The Service was conducted by the Bishop of London, Dr Richard Chartres. His ashes were later placed in Brompton Cemetery.

Dr Jones, his friend and colleague from the Royal College of Surgeons, kept in touch with Martin Israel for the rest of his life, though their careers and lives took separate paths. He recalls their occasional contacts that sometimes revealed unexpected responses from Martin, sometimes warm, at other times frigid, that many others who knew him also experienced from time to time. By pure chance he heard of his ordination into the Church of England in 1974. He and his family decided it would be an appropriate gesture for them all to attend. But when they met later Martin showed extreme displeasure, and said that they should not have gone. What his reasons were for wanting to keep his medical and pastoral duties distinctly apart Dr Jones never knew. But he was surprised to find that Martin had acquired so many new friends in the Church, and was pleased at the respect he was accorded in his new environment.

Some years before, Dr Jones had been facing financial problems arising from events at the IBMS, of a kind that threatened his son's school fees. He happened to mention this to Martin who immediately loaned the £400 that he needed. Later when he went to repay him Martin generously waived the debt. 'I am a single man with no commitments and quite enough for my needs', he said. 'There is no reason for me to have the money back. I am happy to do this for you.'

Later in 1981 Dr Jones needed some help again, this time involving an international medical matter on which he sought some professional assistance from Martin. 'I was surprised when he refused. Such was the firm but neither impolite nor unfriendly nature of the response that I did not ask the reason. Perhaps he felt that danger might lurk with our association, or else he wanted the break with his scientific past to be final; or it might simply have been that he had no access to a microscope.'

Over the years Dr Jones and Martin kept in touch through exchanging Christmas cards. 'On several occasions I called at his flat in Tregunter Road but I never found him in. Matters became easier when he moved south of the river near Battersea Park. In August I used to call upon him with apples from our garden. By that time I was in possession of a simple and radical means of cancer treatment which was also cheap, humane and successful against the majority of malignant conditions. Martin was very sympathetic but it was clear to both of us that the professional world he had once inhabited was too far removed for him to be of help.'

On one of my visits he told me he had been diagnosed with Parkinson's Disease. I was relieved to find that he was being well cared for. He enjoyed the Christmas trips to New Zealand undertaken in his last years. His decline was slow but steady, and on my last two visits on which I called it was not possible to see him.

On the last occasion that we met, he spoke of the physical abuse to which his father had subjected him as a boy. The revelation came as no surprise; years before he had mentioned the matter in passing. When his father was dying in South Africa Martin told me he had gone out to visit the old man. When I was unable to suppress a reaction, his reply indicated that it was natural that he should go. His Christian faith proved much stronger than the painful and unhappy memories his father's selfish, cruel and criminal acts had left him with. But the reserve that had accompanied the earlier admission was no longer there. I was taken aback when he wept openly in front of me. Until that moment I had no idea how fundamentally such experiences can affect the victims. Witnessing his grief shocked me deeply.

In retrospect I realised that apart from the mental wounds there had been a profound effect on Martin as a person, impinging on him in a multiplicity of ways. The suspicion remains that the childhood abuse did irreparable harm to his capacity to form relationships of the kind so many of us are fortunate to be able to take for granted as central and integral parts of our lives. The theme of coping with pain runs like a blood-red streak through his writing, especially in his later work. It is clear too that in reaching out to others in similar positions the intention was to provide comfort for himself as well as for them. Poor, poor Martin; from the incident of his breakdown it is sadly apparent that the healing he experienced personally was meagre, and, if anything, the emotional pain intensified as his life drew to its end.'

Dr Jones concludes, 'As I put down my pen I am struck by regret. Regret that I did not get to know this man better, and that I did not recognise his needs. Regret, too, that I failed to see how closely our perspectives in life interweaved. We took it for granted that life and duty were indivisible and we simply got on with it. We were each intimately concerned with the alleviation of pain; Martin, spiritually, by direct contact with people, and I, physically, initially by working in the laboratory and only later finding myself in a position to help patients directly. Martin's faith equipped him better for the task than I, and visualised service as an extension of his beliefs. In enriching the lives of many he left us ever in his debt'.

Perhaps the closing paragraphs of this brief biography of Martin Israel should be summarised with extracts from the essence of the last of his own writings, the final chapters of *Everlasting Goal* which many readers will not have seen. 'How can we grow up into mature adults as we enter the twenty-first century?' he asks. The first necessity is humility; that we do not know it all, and that the role of servant suits us best. In this role we do not need to compete with one another, since we all have gifts as God has seen fit to give us. The other necessity is love, deep warmth and affection for everyone. It cannot be simulated. It comes from the heart. Inter-faith dialogue becomes stimulating, not for converting people, but to open the mind to another way of perceiving things.

Forgiveness is essential. But it must indeed come from the heart. All human disharmonies will eventually be healed. 'I cannot visualise a heaven that is not universalistic', he affirms. 'The twentieth century's record of murderous dictators, all of whom are God's creatures, are to be accommodated with the saints of humanity. The theme is so vast that it beggars description. The role of the saint in the afterlife is to assist those whose lives on earth have been evil; indeed the saint is doing this now.'

'As we give, so we learn. As we serve so we become masters. We all have qualities of sanctity within ourselves.'

And finally, 'We are all moving towards the everlasting goal even though some of us are making a real mess of it at present. When we all have achieved this we will be in heaven, and the leaders will be Jesus Christ and Gautama Buddha'.

2. Reminiscences

During the preparation of this book we have received a number of letters with reminiscences from people who knew Dr Martin Israel and appreciated his advice and friendship. Some of these have been included in the biographical text as they seemed to contribute directly to the narrative account of his life and work. Others have nonetheless been appreciated and valued. Acknowledgments have been made elsewhere. Selected individual quotations are reproduced here but to avoid possible sensitivities the contributors are not identified.

'Being counselled by Martin Israel was often a disconcerting experience. There were frequent long silences, on occasion lasting the whole of the session. Yet people in their hundreds came to him for spiritual guidance, and few went away disappointed. Why? Because he seemed to have an intuitive (some would say a psychic) understanding of them and of their deepest spiritual needs, which he helped them to sort out at a deeper than verbal level. His lectures and retreat addresses were greatly treasured. He would speak almost as though the words were being given him by some outside source, and he needed no notes to be able to speak for an hour at a time, in complex but perfectly formed sentences. And it was all solid material, without padding and with few illustrative anecdotes. He never promised believers an easy spiritual experience and his honesty in this respect, and his evident spiritual maturity brought him a large following.'

'Martin Israel conducted our wedding service at Holy Trinity, Prince Consort Road, on Tuesday 11 September 1979. Like a later fateful anniversary of that day many years later in another city, it was a beautiful morning with a cloudless sky and the faded warmth of autumn. We were in our mid-twenties and nervous. Not as nervous, it seemed, as Martin himself, who was jumping around the vestry before the event and, on the bride's arrival, he shot off down the aisle in front of her and her surprised father like a gunshot. *(Editor's note – it was fairly early in his ministry!)* As was ever the case, however, when the service was in his hands his personality settled as soon as he began to speak, and when he started to preach he was transformed. We had attended his church for some while and were used to this pattern. His message at our wedding surprised some of our guests. He was tough. Marriage was not going to be easy. We should give up all ideas of being separate units; sharing pain was part of the deal. He remained our advisor (one would hesitate to say 'friend') and we were enormously privileged in that he remembered us in his prayers every day. Our last visit to Martin, with our two children for whom he was godfather, was when he was ill and living in Battersea. Despite his illness he seemed to be possessed of a new calm. The radiance we had experienced before only when he was preaching was now present in his everyday conversation. He blessed all four of us. We were lucky indeed.'

'My husband and I had very happy memories of Fr Martin Israel. We were both members of his Church, Holy Trinity in South Kensington, and we used to manage the monthly book sales and coffee mornings. We often went on his day retreats, especially at Easter, and his silent retreat weekends and healing retreats outside London. He was always compassionate and ready to listen without being judgmental. Whenever he spoke in the pulpit at the Sunday Mass I always felt a special divine presence, as he spoke directly without any notes. He was truly imbibed in the Old Testament and was sincere. At one time when I was teaching O level students both of the palms of my hands broke out into blisters. I consulted Dr Martin at his home, explaining that I was under stress. I opened my hands and he gazed upon them for several seconds saying nothing. I believe he called upon the Holy Spirit. Within a few days the blisters had healed without any medication – a divine miracle. Each evening I hold him in my prayers.'

'The four things I remember about Dr Martin Israel were these: the silences; his retreats; his spiritual guidance; and his gifts as an exorcist, which is often described as "the ministry of deliverance". All very relevant.'

'At the first of Martin's retreats that I attended I had an interview with him. I asked if he would be my spiritual director. He agreed and I benefited from twice yearly visits to him until he died. During these visits I was not intimidated as I expected to be, and he led me on to become more aware of my gifts. His positive encouragement was most enlightening and enabled me to see how I could help other people to live the Christian life. We would have twenty minutes talking then twenty minutes silence. The silence was always profound and helped me in my own contemplation.'

'After my mother's death I was pressurised to get out of our council house and I also needed surgery – I was a mess. Later at a friend's house I saw a man called Dr Martin Israel giving a TV talk and immediately realised that he was the adviser I needed at that time. Later when in London, I saw a talk advertised by him, but it was bad winter weather. Finally I came across a weekend retreat of his and oh what a blessing it was. My second and final retreat with him was unforgettable, with laying on of hands from person to person in complete silence. Initially I felt nothing, but later a heat, the warmth of the Holy Spirit, crept up my neck. It is not easy to put into words. After his illness I would visit him in Battersea. I never felt he was sufficiently appreciated by the Church which often happens when you are "different".'

'In 1998 I told Martin that my husband and I were moving to live in a retirement home for retired clergy and their wives, and that I was alarmed at the thought of living among a lot of clergy. "Don't worry", he replied, "They're not nearly so bad without their dog collars."'

'Martin and I would write to each other and our exchange of letters was bimonthly although he found it a burden to write in the later years. I have very few of these letters but he remains a strength in my life. I read his published work through the later seventies into the eighties and I attended a retreat with him in the 1980s. Subsequently I went to London to visit him for brief meetings. He appeared to enter my emotional life in a caring and sensitive way. From the responses he found there we developed a friendship, a discussion of childhoods, of sharing relationships spiritual and secular. He consolidated this in his care for my professional development and he attempted to encourage my greater involvement in theology and religious affairs, community, and finally in a more engaged political – institutional stance. I could not do justice to this prompting! From these promptings towards external worldly affairs I feel that he discerned I needed a more balanced life. However I have always been a rather reclusive private individual, despite my family, wife and children and teaching career. Martin's strength was the ability to relate to all of this and remain firmly rooted in the worlds of faith and state. The one phrase I will share with you that he wrote is “Yes your friendship is important to me. It allows amongst my desperate situation for me to remain cheerful”.’

‘I had been reading a book by Martin at Hilfield Friary. I mentioned it to someone while washing up. “Oh, I know Martin” said one of the friars; “I'll give you his address”. I wrote to him and asked if I could come and see him. He wrote back within the week with an invitation. He subsequently became my spiritual director and friend. He was a great encourager: “Of course you will be ordained, it's exactly the right thing for you”, and on visiting him with my girlfriend, “Of course you two will be married!” I am now ordained. We did get married and have two children. Martin always helped me to see the way ahead, and encouraged me to take the next step.’

‘The reputation of Martin Israel first came to my attention in 1993 when I was at the Christian Meditation Centre in Kensington. I had heard that he was a deeply spiritual man who preached from the heart and was compelling to listen to. So one Sunday morning I went to his parish to listen to him and was greatly impressed. He did exactly as I hoped he would. I wasn't disappointed and I suppose what struck me then was the range of subjects he took in, and human suffering was very much part of it. In 1994 I became a novice at Worth Abbey and found myself again led to Martin through the spiritual friendship of a parishioner. I listened to a lot of his talks on tape and managed to get to a retreat he gave at the nearby Sayers Common community. Following on from that I got to know Martin in my own right and for the space of about five years he became my spiritual confidant and director. I would visit him at his home in Battersea and I would often contact him by phone. The time during which I saw Martin was a key time for my spiritual growth. I was taking solemn profession vows into my Benedictine community and I was also being ordained into priestly ministry. However, more pertinently, there were also big changes going on within me. “My” internal energy was starting to rise and open me up interiorly. The different chakras were starting to come to life and change the way I perceived God's presence. This was a very challenging time and in a way no-one in a conventional theological way had prepared me for it. I therefore used to talk over a lot of the effects with Martin, seeking guidance and reassurance which he was always able to give me. Also he encouraged me to continue on this path and to see God's presence in it. I remember one particular instance, which was the first time I was attacked by an outside negative force. It was the first time that anything like this had happened to me and was particularly frightening. I phoned up the next day and spoke to Martin and after a pause in which he told me he was going to "ask" about it, he was able to confirm to me that it was "a particularly unpleasant spiritual entity". He then passed on the advice to me of how to deal with it, which was "take it to the community", which was something I really did not want to do. In the end much to my relief it only led to me having a psychological assessment and also having a rather interesting session with a local cranial osteopath. I always got the impression that Martin was preparing me for my current role of exercising a priestly and healing ministry. He had great wisdom and great humility as well. His sessions were very gentle and he had a lovely habit of following up any real bit of wisdom he imparted to me by saying (with a smile), "of course, I might be totally deluded". Whenever he said that I knew he had just said something really important. Towards the end of his life, regrettably, I lost touch with him as I spent more time away, but I always remember him with much affection and count it as a great blessing to me that our lives touched.'

'We had the great privilege of Martin's friendship, having met him in 1990 via a mutual friend. Martin gave us kindly and helpful advice on personal matters and we invited him and his delightful New Zealand carers several times down to our farm in Sussex, where we and our sons spent many illuminating hours in his company, both benefiting from his great wisdom and also enjoying periods of silence together. He had a particular affinity with our eldest son Tim who had several long conversations with him both here and in London. We also heard him preach at Holy Trinity Church in London and I still have copies of many of his sermons recorded in the parish newsletters, which still make excellent reading. When I suffered an accident in France and had to spend a month in hospital I was so touched and pleased to receive a telephone call from him there. I had with me there his book *A Light on the Path* which I found illuminating. He was a very private person, so such personal care that he accorded us was hugely appreciated. When staying with us in Sussex he slept in an old four poster bed (installed in our family home by my father who collected rare and wonderful objects). This bed is enormous and decorated with the Medici shields. Martin divined that there was a troubled spirit linked to that bed which he helped on its spiritual journey.'

'Martin Israel came to see me shortly before we moved house. We made instant and profound contact and he stayed for several hours. I felt I had known him since the world began. When the world finally gets "one gospel" who can foretell what will follow? On one occasion he said to me: "One day I shall be Martin Christ and you will be Diana Christ".'

'I was in limbo travelling from agnosticism to some kind of faith. My husband went shopping and left me in the car with a heap of books. One of these was *The Pain that Heals* by Martin Israel. It completed my conversion and I read the rest of his publications. I wrote and asked him if he would see me. His reply shook me a little, "I have been expecting you". On one visit I asked him, "If I visited you and neither of us spoke a word, might I still be carried forward?" He answered "Yes, but you've come all the way from Cornwall and that warrants words!"'

'I was introduced to Martin by a priest friend who suggested him as a mentor in my work as a Christian doctor. He became a "soul friend" to my wife and myself until he became too ill to continue. We also knew Geraldine, the Christian sensitive who worked closely with Martin at that time. They helped us in a steep and often painful learning curve in understanding certain psychic phenomena in our practice.'

'Upon hearing about this book I was filled with joy but also an immense sadness. Martin and I had been only children, neither of us English, and we used to joke about being brother and sister as it were. On his retreats I always felt like a bird that had found its nest. I have some sixty or so of his letters...'

‘I joined the Churches’ Fellowship in the mid nineteen-sixties, during the period when Frances Banks was a Council member, and this brought to an end a solitary search for answers to my questions on life after death following a bereavement. I felt I had come home, and was in the company of like-minded people. Martin belonged in this circle, having just begun his career as a speaker on spiritual matters. I began by being in awe of him and not being at ease, but over a period of years we became good friends, and I recognised the struggle he had with his temperament. I regularly visited him in Battersea.’

‘I met Dr Martin Israel at a local Catholic convent where he gave retreats. My daughter had been diagnosed with persistent manic-depression, and I had gone to a number of healing services which gave hope. But it was Martin who really helped me grasp the nettle and accept that she might not be healed in the way I was hoping this side of eternity, though medication in the right balance might help. His compassion was apparent and he promised to pray for me. The last time I spoke to him I described a beatific dream I had had of my beloved father, who had died many years ago at the age of 45, intimating all was well. Martin simply told me that my father wished to communicate to me, and I believe that was true.’

‘I was wondering what had happened to my friend and mentor Martin S. Israel, and since 2007 I had hoped a letter would reach me in far off Maine USA in reply to recent Christmas cards. I had corresponded with him since 1981 when I read *Summons to Life*. I sent him a cassette of church music and he expressed himself willing to write from time to time. Martin in his writings emphasised Love and Stewardship. There were only positives in his assumptions, and this led me to the phrase “Caring Love” which I used in my own written testimony, using extensive quotes from Martin for which he did not rebuke me. I was never able to meet him personally but I did once telephone him for a brief Christmas greeting.’

‘Through Martin and his knowledge of the next life I have come to view death as birth into a new freer life and to see it as an extension of this life, taking away fear and giving understanding. This helped so much when my husband unexpectedly died. To Martin I owe so much.’

‘Martin was a very good friend during the sixties and seventies when still at the Royal College of Surgeons. On one occasion when his profession came up in discussion he referred to his patients as his friends.’

‘Martin came into my life when my mother was struck down with schizophrenia. For two harrowing years we watched her descend into a nightmare world of “voices”. We heard of Martin Israel on the radio and wrote to him. He replied saying he had “looked into the matter” and found my mother surrounded by darkness. He would give her absent healing. My mother immediately experienced two days of calm, and only later did I tell her about Martin Israel. From then onward whenever his name was mentioned she would feel calm and strengthened. If a bad attack came on I would write and he would respond at once. Then we found a psychiatrist who was able to prescribe the right medicine. Martin later became my spiritual director and I would visit him in Battersea. His silences could be daunting but his smile relaxed me and his humour was delightful. He spoke of his early life and suffering. Would he have changed anything? No, for otherwise he could not have helped people in the way he did. And he said his work would continue on the other side!’

‘Like others I had some spiritual experiences which changed my life, and about which I needed guidance that at the time I could not get from my local church. I found a study group in London to which Martin belonged, and I began seeing him monthly for spiritual direction. I remember especially his gift for listening. He rarely gave any verbal direction. He just reassured me with regard to the path I was following and the way in which I was trying to deal with any difficulties. He would give correction if necessary. He seemed to know me thoroughly; and he completely and lovingly accepted me. It taught me a great deal.’

‘I met Martin on one of the many retreats he gave and was immediately aware that he was not only a gifted speaker but also possessed unique spiritual qualities – and Christ-like qualities of healing and selfless love for others. I remember him each day and am confident that he is still reaching out to help his friends. I remember that he always accompanied me to the door at the end of our meetings. Two of his remarks remain in my memory: "I have always liked you ...!" and "Why has it taken you so long ...?".'

'I first encountered Dr Martin Israel when, as a medical student at Birmingham, I read "Walter and Israel" on Pathology, an accessible and comprehensive introduction to the phenomenon of disease. Thirty years later I met him through a friend, together with another friend of mine who was Russian, an iconographer, and a pious and reverent Orthodox who had been unjustly bullied by another ecclesiastic. Yet my Russian friend sensed that Martin, an Anglican priest, was deeply orthodox within her meaning of the word. She equated him with the spiritual directors or *staretzi* of her own church. There was something about Martin Israel that transcended doctrine so that people of other faiths or denominations, or of no faith at all, could relate to him without threat of indoctrination or judgement. He had trained as a scientist and a pathologist – a discipline requiring intellectual rigour. I like to call such people "phenomenologists", a term applicable to all who study natural or supernatural phenomena. Martin was able to describe such things both subjectively and objectively in a way that was true for all of us.'

'He held a conviction that within everyone there was universality, and this phenomenon was his study and practice. Contemplation and disclosed experience informed his thought and theology. His teaching and his ministry of healing was to this purpose and to direct us to "that of God in Everyman".'

'*The Pain that Heals* looked an interesting book, at a time when I was painfully debating whether or not to seek ordination. *Crockford's Directory* put me in touch with the author at his Church, and there began a friendship that lasted from 1986. I have notes of relaxed, friendly, smiling visits over the years, and assurances that he was praying for me constantly. His advice was practical: anxiety and depression are not profitable, and much depression is caused by the chemistry of the brain. Towards the end of his life his voice became very quiet and gentle. He offered one afternoon for us to meet and pray – this was real prayer! I felt my back involuntarily straighten and my body lift up in the chair. He was pleased to know that his praying still had power. This was the last time I met him.'

'Extract from a letter written by Martin to a friend: "Man's great work is himself. His place of operation is wherever he finds himself, and his tools are the means at hand. There is no thing greater than another. Nothing high or low. Each experience is a stepping-stone toward completion. The key-note of constructive living is Balance."'

'Thank you for all your letters, Martin, your addresses, your television appearances (where I first encountered your quietly spoken wealth of wisdom), your books of course, and for writing in one of them, "Hold fast to the good, the true and the beautiful, and nothing can harm you", and also for what you told me at a Canterbury Conference: "Do not put any impediment between yourself and the Holy Spirit."'

3. Reflections on his Published Works

Martin Israel published the first of his spiritual books in 1974. He soon became a celebrated writer in this field, notably among the clergy of many denominations. Some people came to know him for his writings alone. He wrote as he preached, intensely and inspirationally. Each sentence or paragraph introduces a fresh theme or a new approach, often with an academic turn of phrase reflecting his training as a medical doctor and lecturer in pathology. His concern was always to strive for professionalism in a field that is all too often overlaid with dogmatism at one extreme, and emotion at the other. Anyone who has sought to edit, transcribe, or reproduce any of his works will recall the strictness of the author as editor, proof reader and punctuator of his own material. Consequently a compiler attempting to construct a summary of his works or a précis, faces an immediate challenge: how to do justice to the material and yet to conclude with an end result that is comprehensive, yet shorter than the original, and above all to ensure that it is still acceptable to Dr Israel himself.

We have resolved not to attempt the task. The following passages are offered as a way-in to Martin Israel's books, in the hope that the reader will be sufficiently inspired to obtain the original works and to study them directly. They are no more than reflections of the original. Martin Israel is not always an 'easy read' and for this reason we are offering shorter sentences and briefer paragraphs. Some of his themes involve intricate philosophy and analysis of spiritual or mystical concepts. Here we have tried to keep it simple, and in some cases have opted out altogether. So what of the choice of material, of what to put in and what to leave out? And how about the turn of phrase and the use of language? In each of these respects you are in the compiler's hands, and hopefully also in the hands of God. We hope they will challenge, interest and motivate you to study more deeply the writings of one whom the compiler feels to be of special relevance today. Martin Israel is surely in the ancient tradition of the English Mystics – notably Dame Julian of Norwich, whose sayings appear often in his writings.

4. Summons to Life - The Search for Identity through the Spiritual

First published in 1974, this work is one of the earliest of Martin Israel's spiritual writings. Mankind struggles to keep alive, he affirms. We are obsessed with acquiring things, yet we seldom have the time or the understanding to enjoy them. The will to survive is essential for our earthly survival, yet if our sole object is to escape death or to postpone it, we are effectively dead already. Are we concerned primarily with wealth, or fame, or power, or the approval of others? Or do we have a will to pursue the true meaning of life which leads us on from the mere physical to mental growth, and so onward to spiritual understanding? This book deals with the spirit of mankind, what it is and how it may be experienced. When we come to know ourselves we can experience true liberation from material things and can then begin to live with purpose and meaning. This is the life abundant and those who have it can never die.

The Measure of a Human Being

How hard it is to define a human being. Humanity cannot be confined to the body, nor to the reasoning mind and the emotions, which may fluctuate and in themselves may not greatly distinguish us from the higher animals, apart perhaps from our ability to manipulate the outside world. It is when we move beyond mere selfish gratification that we begin to experience the true depths of our nature. The mind can then run free. We may thus experience hope and our hearts expand. 'Know thyself' is the ancient Delphic motto of wisdom. When we know ourselves we grow into life.

But what is the essence of ourselves? I am the result of conditioning begun by my parents. Without the conditioning of education I cannot be truly effective. Moreover I am the product of my genetic inheritance, whatever that may amount to, driving me to seek self-preservation, sexual gratification, and to fulfil other motives both conscious and unconscious which may precede or hinder growth and self-actualisation.

It is when we have to make some important moral choice in our lives, however, that we begin to discover ourselves. There may be pain and suffering all around us, but when we have to cast aside conformity and convention to do something which we know to be right, then we register our authentic nature. We become more fully ourselves so that our nature shines forth and our body itself is transmuted.

Mankind grows in stature through making these moral choices, which is why self-realisation often comes through suffering. The suffering itself is brought about by a false idea of ourselves, which is hard to avoid because of the conditioning of our everyday material lives. From this essentially selfish self to the true spiritual self, which is our true identity, is a long way.

The main attributes of the soul are its all-embracing nature and its wide range. The soul does not seek for itself alone; it is never selfish. Its joy is the joy of all creation. The body is the vehicle of the soul, mirroring the inner nature of the person. Thus it is that a soul-infused body is seen most often in little children. Subsequent experience may dull the soul and darken the body unless the child experiences love.

When we live in a materialistic environment we tend to be controlled by outer events which may give us inner disquiet. Within this darker world we work only to survive. But this is not the life that we were destined to lead. We have fallen from our birthright in a vain attempt to gain comfort or reassurance from possessions. The more insecure we feel the worse it gets. The more I need to have, the less I truly am. But the less concerned I am about my well-being, and the more I flow outward to the world, the richer I am.

The more I am able to flow outward in this way, the stronger becomes the spirit within me, but so often I am worn down by the cares of this mortal life. When however I am able to overcome this distress I am able to perceive the being of God and so progress to the most exciting quest – the pursuit of the spiritual ascent.

The Spirit of God leads us into the truth about ourselves, our true self-knowledge. To be fully oneself is the greatest joy one can know, for at last we are free. This freedom may be gained at a heavy price but when we are free we can enjoy our own being as well as the world around us. This spirituality – often mistakenly confused with religion –

gives us inner acknowledgement of our true nature and our destination.

How can we know God? Simply by living in the present moment and responding positively to those around us and the challenges they might bring. This is spirituality – no longer to be thought of as the preserve of the religious. The journey into our own inner nature is also the way to God. In this lies eternal joy.

The Point of Departure

Where do we start on our spiritual journey? There is no one answer. A child is in some ways more aware of the world and its wonders than the seasoned adult, dulled by the illusions of the material world. But this is not the whole answer. For the child is a passive spectator whereas the adult becomes a mature participator.

Our first impulse is to survive. We cannot grow until our immediate needs have been met. Yet in addition we need to be recognised as a person when we are still little, each with our own name. Many children are not properly acknowledged as separate individuals by their own parents, and this gives them difficulty, for they do not then know who they really are. The love of the parent identifies each person and allows for the development of the contented child, which permits our progress into ultimate union with God. This view is of course incomplete, since much of childhood is of necessity self-centred. Also it is inadequate, for it depends upon a favourable environment in the outside world, without which the contentment is soon destroyed.

The growth into a greater knowledge of God is not imposed upon us but is learned by experience. It requires the dedication of every part of our personality. There are no pre-conditions other than a humble willingness to accept life, and a faith that persists in adversity.

We need to strip ourselves of the illusions that surround us. This is rarely by choice but is brought upon us by events we might call tragedies, or at the very least disappointments. The role of suffering is vital in the process of personal growth, but we need to know how to confront it. It is no use someone telling us our suffering is good for us, even though this may be true. The key is for us to admit that we can of ourselves do nothing. The courage to take this step opens the way shown to Dame Julian of Norwich, that sin is necessary but that finally all will be well.

Sin is our natural state. It is a condition in which we pursue the devices and desires of our own hearts in preference to those which may bring about the greater good. Yet we were made in the image of God which makes it possible for us to work in collaboration with the Creator, albeit by a supreme effort. This collaboration marks out the spiritual life. It never offers us an easy path but we are given the strength and insight to guide us.

And we are aided along the way. It is said that every petition or prayer we make in faith is heard and answered, even though this may not be obvious at the time. ‘Ask and you shall receive’, ‘knock and it shall be opened to you’. What is needed from us is the confidence to forge ahead knowing that in time this help will come, despite evidence to the contrary.

It is also said that all creatures live in psychic communion. Hence any sin that we commit, meaning an action that exalts us above our fellows, excludes us from the spirit of life that animates the world. We need to confess the act and seek forgiveness, and if through pride or ignorance we fail to do this, then eventually our mind and body will suffer.

Paradoxically the more I grow into maturity the less I rely upon my own talents and the more I look towards that which is beyond me. The power that is beyond me enables me to grow more into my true being and so to become more useful. This is my initial and my final encounter with God, which is here defined not as an idolised father-figure, but as 'that which is'. The more I acknowledge my weakness the stronger I become. The more I realise I can do nothing, the more I can achieve without fatigue. The fruit of spirituality is an analysis of our attributes so that our true self can be revealed and we can detach ourselves from reliance on those things that are not of God.

It must be said that not all growth is obtained by tragedy or adversity. We may also grow by unpretentiously following the path that is set before us. God is with us in all places provided we have the courtesy to pay attention.

The Vale of Enlightenment

True knowledge comes to us in our everyday life. It comes like a thief in the night, when least expected. It transforms our perception of things, provided we have awareness. It can bring us inner stillness, of a kind we can bring into our world of work, not merely to be relegated to periods of prayer or meditation.

As I lose myself in commitment to others, so I find my true self. As I release myself from the bondage of self-concern I do not escape from the world. Rather I identify more closely with the world around me. Hence Jesus' statement that he who would save his life shall lose it, but he who loses himself for the sake of others shall have the eternal life that comes from the true realisation of identity.

Thus we are all members one of another. Once I can rise above self-centredness I can never be alone and I can hope for salvation. Yet this does not come by direct seeking. The more we press for self-enlightenment the more we are likely to fail. Anything that boosts the personality and enhances our power over others will separate us from the rest of mankind. But anything that diminishes the claims of the personality brings us into fuller communion with the process of life. We need to adopt an attitude of harmlessness. To love someone else we must first be aware of that person and respect their identity.

'He who has the Son, has life' says St John in his first epistle. We all have the Son though only a few are aware of it, and it is these who can bear witness. But first they have to be prepared, and they do this by serving their neighbour. Hence we all have to learn the second great commandment – to love our neighbour as our self. By serving our neighbour we come to know God, so that the second commandment is an extension of the first: we then become able to love God with all our heart.

The presence of God

An awareness of God is not the end of the path to spirituality. It is merely an important milestone. We progress by trusting that good will prevail in the end, and often when we are most sorely tested God appears to us. Whatever is said about God is wrong. He transcends all the categories into which we place him. Despite this he comes to us as person to person. The awareness of God is an awareness of warmth, that tells us of a power that cares for us as we are, and loves us for what we may be. This warmth opens us to the potentialities that lie within us. I am loved for what I am and my sins are forgiven me. This does not mean that the past and its consequences suddenly cease, but it does mean that they no longer imprison me. They can become lessons from which I can learn, and I can learn compassion towards others.

But not everything is straightforward. When someone experiences the love of God at the emotional peak of a revivalist meeting of the wrong kind, where wickedness is loudly denounced, they may all too easily equate forgiveness from sin with the holding of a rigid and dogmatic religious position. They then become imprisoned within a small class of the 'elect' or 'the saved', which separates them from a true understanding of the providence of God. If ever we are unwise enough to believe we have the whole answer to God's being, we immediately shut Him out of our lives and we deceive ourselves. On the other hand, anything given us that is truly of God is by definition perfect. It offers us growth into greater awareness, and the test of our personal integrity begins.

The dynamics of salvation

To the over-simplistic person, salvation is a state of purification which happens suddenly and once accepted it is complete. The recipient perceives themselves as one of the 'saved', and among the 'sheep' of the Bible as against the 'goats' who are condemned. Then follows a period when the 'saved' become priggish in attitude, and presume to preach or condescend to their fellows. For they have a set of rules and attitudes that will lead them straight to God. Often they are imbued with a missionary zeal that may have as much to do with inner uncertainties and the needs of their ego as to a deep feeling for their fellows. They know it all and cannot wait to propagate it.

True salvation is the healing of the whole personality. It is the integration of body, mind and emotion, under the direction of God through our souls. It is a slow and progressive process. It is punctuated by episodes of failure which themselves can be turned to advantage through God's grace. Thus did Christ spend time in the wilderness following a rugged path through desolation to enlightenment. It is a far cry from the arrogance of those apparently redeemed souls who thank God that they are not as others are. It involves self-discovery which comes to us as we forget ourselves and become involved in the world around us. We do not need a wilderness in which to find it; it is all around us in the bustle of a big modern city. Firstly we must relate to others. Then we must pursue our vocation whatever it may be. And lastly we must be prepared to suffer, which is a part of the human condition.

Spiritual growth in everyday life

The lives of most of us who aspire to the spiritual life swing between quiet contemplation and hectic modern everyday life. This may seem to rule out real spiritual progress. Religious communities exist as an apparent path for those with the right vocation. It is all too easy to blame my life for my lack of spiritual advancement. How can I advance when daily life offers me no respite? It calls for an attitude of detached awareness and a determination to give of my best to the day's task however taxing or boring it may be. This is not easy and we may be led into lack of commitment for a variety of reasons. One of the more difficult can be friction with others in the workplace, repercussions of which can take over the course of our lives. A state of willed awareness is called for. We have to recognise what is happening. It is important that our attention should flow out to the work, to endeavour to rest whilst working vigorously, to relax in the heat of activity.

It is often said that tension can be creative, and indeed tension is an inevitable feature of a material world. But the key to an unfolding of latent talents is a sense of balance. Once there is calm, the work of the

Spirit can proceed.

Meditation in action

Despite our best laid plans, things go wrong. The unexpected takes over and becomes the master of events. But if we can accept each moment as it comes as a challenge or sacrament in itself, we can assert self-control over the event and accept it as part of our process of growth. This is called 'meditation in action' in the Buddhist tradition. It does not mean accepting fate in a spineless way but rather an active participation through a willed giving of oneself. Then a purpose behind the event can often be perceived. And through this purpose and the weakness in which we find ourselves God can reveal Himself. A mind that is quiet and at peace and yet is committed in a detached way is at the very heart of the spiritual life. It is important to understand this, because it is only when we are in this state that we can receive the love of God, without which we cannot truly pass that love to another.

When we try and reach a decision in our daily life we try to aim for a successful outcome, yet often without really knowing what will comprise success. In front of us may lie uncertainty. Thus it is faith rather than reason which will lead us through 'the valley of the shadow of death'. And that faith is of God.

Ideas of good and evil, essential as they are in practice, can become merely relative. For compassion can change evil into good, whereas condemnation merely hardens and crystallises the negative impulse. As we obey the summons to life we come face to face with love – a most fundamental experience.

The mystery of love

Love is what joins our souls to God. We are never complete when we are alone, and we seek companionship. When we are young this often takes the form of 'falling in love', with all its violent emotions that often defy reason. But for many people it is an essential part of their development.

The beauty of this condition is that it causes us to forget ourselves and instead to project our concerns on to the beloved. Life takes on a new meaning. But falling in love is also confusing and even deluding in some ways. Self is eclipsed but so also is judgement, and this can lead to many difficulties. It is easy to be cynical about 'young love' but this is wrong on every level. Until you give yourself and experience betrayal you cannot know what your soul amounts to. A fool in love is a fool for God. Whatever is lost is repaid by increased self-knowledge.

But romantic love has to pass and to be replaced by something more substantial. When it is anchored in something more substantial such as marriage it loses much of its glamour. A constant relationship where home truths are perceived and shared can be a fearful experience but also a healing one. Facing up to our own shortcomings teaches us more about ourselves, which we cannot achieve without first giving of ourselves. On the other hand there are many unions – possibly most unions – where these true relationships do not develop. The partners simply do not know each other. But how beautiful a real marriage is to behold!

Not all lovers experience a full relationship. Some become so attached to one another that they become chained so that neither is truly free. In due course one of them must die and the other must mourn. If this mourning continues too long the identity of the bereaved cannot reassert itself. This is not the fruit of a true love – the love of Christ.

True love is the growing into maturity of both partners. This kind of love makes no demands. It does not seek results. It knows that ultimately all will be well, even during darkness and suffering.

Love in action

When love is being given and received The Holy Spirit is working. John the Baptist speaks of his own eclipse as the power of Jesus grows. This is love in action, which may lead to one of us giving their whole lives for another. There might be a complete surrender of the earthly personality, but the soul rises triumphant.

In this understanding of true love we can glimpse our mature relationship with God. But then we have to resume our duties on earth and the radiance is lost. Yet as we progress, we may be more fully aware of the Infinite. In a true relationship with God there can be no turning back, for we become able to know Him and do not need to prove anything. We grow in maturity whilst , nonetheless, not wishing to be put to the test until we are able.

Mature love is not emotional. It is a quiet contemplation centred on the beloved. But this does not mean that love is blind. It acknowledges the evil around it without being repelled. For we come to know the love of God by actively dedicating ourselves to the world around us. Even our early love affairs provide a gateway. Later we learn compassion for the afflicted and when we reach the intensity of berating God for this universal suffering, then we learn to pray.

Love and human relationships

'Thou shall love thy neighbour as thyself' because he or she indeed is thyself. But this love requires experience and realism, not blinding ourselves to the imperfect. Detached commitment is the secret and it may take years to perfect. Some people we instinctively like, others we feel neutral about, and a few we actively dislike. Yet we have to show love for them all without demanding that they change to accord with us. This calls for attentiveness and prayer to God.

The role of conflict is an important one. It leads to growth, and there comes a time when truth must override politeness, but although we must assess the other person, we should not judge. This is not for us. Love should be distinguished from mere liking. To develop love calls for willed attention, honesty and quiet receptiveness. We need to listen and learn rather than to converse. In personal relationships we need to be forgiving. Though there may be discord we should never be despairing of anyone, nor yet exalt them too highly. People change, and especially in response to unexpected challenges or difficulties. As always the sin of pride is what can bedevil human relationships, and we should always beware of it. But we should also accept that not every difficult relationship is going to be mended in this life. Rising above such difficulties can lead to personal growth.

An important part of human relationship is the married state, where ideally there is both the physical and the spiritual. In modern times the physical may be given too much attention, and sex separated from love. This can lead to serial relationships which belie a true commitment to the beloved. Complete trust and liberty should be the end and purpose of marriage.

Trust and liberty is also the end of the celibate life, though this can be the harder path and should be only undertaken by those for whom it is intended. 'I must be about my Father's business' in celibacy is not for everyone, though it can bring rich rewards.

The role of suffering

Living is not a static process. There is tumult on the way. It must be said that there is no truly satisfactory explanation as to why we suffer, with an all-loving God. It may help to start with a hypothesis that we have free will, and free will gives us the option to select wrong paths and the evils they bring. It is our destiny to work with God to bring about the best that we can, and the decrying of some committed atheists does not change the situation.

Suffering takes many forms. The simplest relate to the loss of material benefits. The most complex relate to forms of despair, as 'the dark night of the soul'. When we serve God we are tested. For some the path to God appears beatific and is all too easily related to such philosophies as 'positive thinking'. But this, though not necessarily wrong, is not the whole truth.

The pilgrim who passes through the 'dark night' is being given a new understanding of reality, but many of the normal comforts and reassurances are of no account in the process. The mystics describe God as 'that which is'. The more we are like God the more we are in our essence and therefore do not have to exert ourselves. The suffering that leads to a heightened awareness of God is part of the journey to the light. It is never sought, nor is it to be connected to wrong actions in the past.

The inner life

Part of our life is always lived in solitude. The inner life is the part of us with which we learn to know and to accept ourselves. We cannot love another until we have first learned to love ourselves. This truth is not always understood by the conventionally religious person who has been taught to regard themselves as a miserable sinner. Happily we now benefit from modern psychology which can assist our understanding. To love yourself is to accept yourself as you are and to thank God for what you may be. This does not imply self-satisfaction or conceit but an openhearted acceptance of what we are, both the good and the bad. The more we understand our weaknesses the more compassion we can show to others, especially those with similar shortcomings.

In many ways it is our defects that show us the way to God. Our talents, if we are not very careful, can cause us to become puffed up with our own self-worth and this can be a hindrance in our spiritual progress, even some of our seemingly spiritual or 'religious' gifts. Anything which exalts the personality diminishes the soul, and vice-versa. Once we have recognised and acknowledged our weaknesses we can call upon divine help to enlighten our darkness. The self has to be lost so that the soul may develop. A disinterested seeking for God is what nourishes the soul.

To approach God, the mind must be quiet. Inner silence is sometimes called meditation, though not all meditation is of the right kind. The body must be at ease, and stilled and in comfort. The mind must also be quiet, and this may be achieved by reciting a suitable phrase or mantra. Union is sought with the universal body of Christ. When this is achieved there is communion with all other souls. This cannot be mastered by techniques, which can merely exalt the personality. The purpose is a form of self-annihilation which is known as contemplation. Then you begin to know yourself better. But it is not a withdrawal from the world. On the contrary one is fully alive and able to help others. To be able to help others we must have a detachment that allows us to be objective, but we must also have commitment. We must have the perception to know when to say 'no' as well as to have a keenness to help.

Communion with people then becomes possible because we have no need to be self-assertive. We can approach God directly, which is the culmination of the development of the inner way.

Prayer

Prayer is the supreme action of the inner way. It is the communion of the soul with God. It starts with a conscious elevation to God, but when your prayer life is fully established you are never far from the divine presence no matter what you are doing.

With prayer a person is giving themselves to God in silence. Most church services have liturgies of one sort or another that can hinder private prayer in silence, for which there may be no opportunity. In the Hindu-Buddhist tradition, which is more advanced than Western faiths in the inner life of the spirit, various disciplines are employed within the general system of yoga.

Prayer starts with the recognition that there is a supreme being who can be approached in time of difficulty. It commences with oneself and one's needs. It needs no special training, though the kind of petitionary prayer which focuses on our stated needs, interests, and even presumes to prescribe the solutions, is of little or no value and merely distracts the petitioner from the essence of prayer which is the practice of the presence of God. Petitionary prayer does indeed move the seeker away from the mundane, but in other respects it can be at the foothills of the prayer life. For praying is not the same as 'saying our prayers'. In silent prayer the communion that exists between God and all creation becomes tangible to the soul. And when we pray for another we are including them in that communion, not merely asking them to be forgiven for their sins, an essentially presumptuous idea. Prayer is of love. It is selfless. It leads all into freedom. The fruit of prayer is vision. The action of prayer is love.

Prayer and guidance

Suppose that we have a momentous decision to make. It is essential that we take the 'right' step. There is no clear rational solution in which we have trust. So we pray for divine guidance, and what do we get? We may receive a voice that instructs, but is this from God or from some other source? Those with psychic or spiritualistic tendencies may well be prey to unreliable inspiration, and they should beware. But there is one other source – the guidance of the Holy Spirit. He leads us to the truth of the situation, not in a dictatorial way, nor by prescribing exact courses of action. Instead he suffuses our soul with love and wisdom so that as mature beings we can select the right course for ourselves. When we are guided in this way we may have the confidence to trust in divine providence, doing the best we can and leaving the outcome to God. This is what prayer enables.

This is also important in considering 'the gifts of the spirit' brought to greater prominence in recent years by the charismatic movement. If you want to be tractable to the Holy Spirit you must indeed give of yourself, but not to the extent of abandoning reason and sound judgement, your intellect. St Paul reminds us of the three great gifts of faith, hope and love, the greatest of which is love. Petitionary prayer is always heard but we need to be mindful of what we pray for. All prayer centred upon personal development without reference to the greater body of mankind tends to be divisive. When the kingdom of God is sought in the right way all manner of requests will be granted.

The agnosticism of real faith

Our worldly life is a journey towards a visionary goal which is not illuminated by reason. Hence it is not surprising that many intellectuals adopt a sceptical attitude to all matters of faith and religion. This restricts mankind to a life on this earth terminated by total extinction. Religion is merely an opiate to give us the illusion of purpose and destination. 'Without vision the people perish' however. By contrast the religionist has a lively faith, as demonstrated by the many groups that have flourished over the ages, with varying degrees of enlightenment. Faith is not a short cut to salvation. It is a gift from God, in response to prayer, which guides the personality on the path to healing. The spiritual quest is a continuous act of faith, to enable us to move through the tempests of everyday life confident that in the end all will be well.

Real faith develops the personality and makes it more mature. It does not call for the denial of the body or the mind or the emotions.

This is where certain kinds of authoritarian religion can be harmful. True faith does not imprison. A ray of light in a dark world must always be acknowledged, but not without a measure of agnosticism or 'not knowing' which may cause us to pause and examine its source.

Faith and suggestion

Psychology teaches that suggestions placed into the mind can themselves produce results. The doctor's well-known 'bedside manner' can itself benefit the patient, as can the various forms of 'positive thinking' that are practised today by counsellors, mentors and others. Some of these techniques can detract from the independent self-development of the personality, though they may have their place when we are subject to periods of extreme stress. Our endeavour should be to move on from these techniques when the need for the 'first-aid' that they supply has diminished.

Religious faith and spirituality

If religion were doing what it should do, it would bring mankind into an encounter with God. Not all churches succeed in doing this, for a variety of reasons, and many spiritually aware people find God in the world at large. Churches should be the places in which the perplexities of the religious life are addressed and eased, yet all too often they become enmeshed in the kind of organisational politics that assail so many human institutions.

It is and always was the function of the Holy Spirit to lead people into the truth, and organisations often cannot stand this. The Spirit selects all manner of people to help in this work, and from every walk of life, including some militant atheists! It is a sad historic fact that the Western World, in its search for the Christian God, has committed itself to many hideous wars and persecutions, far more than in the Hindu-Buddhist movements of the East, where there is a greater mystical awareness. In the religious quest for Western truth religionists have unhesitatingly persecuted those whom they define as 'heretics'.

Yet the real quest is for the whole truth, which is in God. And whole religion is the religion which brings fullness of being to the person. This is brought by love, not by mere thought. Yet there is value in true religion since it brings the knowledge and experience of others through the years. As we allow the Holy Spirit to lead us so we shall the better understand the eternal meaning of the religions and scriptures.

In assessing religious faith we must beware of two pitfalls. One of these is a slavish adherence to fundamentalist dogma, however persuasive, ignoring the groans of our reasoning minds. The other is to be seduced into feeling we have to be modern and 'with it' either for its own sake or to accord with latest scientific or philosophical thought. Spiritual truth never denies or contradicts reason.

The creeds and sacraments of the Church are not to be dismissed but should be respected. They express eternal truth, but they are not static.

Our spiritual faith will lead us into truth, if we proceed with a humble heart and an adventurous spirit. Externally imposed religious systems may not help us, in which case they are redundant, especially if they 'quench the spirit'.

The social roots of the spirit

It is sometimes critically asserted that the quest for spiritual enlightenment takes us away from the real world into a cocooned environment of our own. There are of course those for whom an enclosed religious life is clearly their vocation, which is a special calling requiring attributes which should in no way be belittled. I am however writing as lay person to lay person.

Anyone living today can only be aware of the immense problems facing us owing to the ambivalence of human nature. There is population growth, disease, malnutrition, over-population, birth control, all of which call forth responses which leave us with a degraded view of humanity. Are we merely a race controlled by sex and the demands of materialism? The growth of Western affluence and the levelling of social division have nonetheless left us with educated young people who have no immediate work or inspiration to look forward to. To avoid the aimlessness of much in modern society they turn to drugs, to pseudo-mystical sects, and even to crime. Will increasing automation give people the leisure for self-development or will they destroy themselves by vice? It depends upon their witness and faith.

These immense problems are outside the scope of any one person or group to solve. They stem from the essential self-centredness of mankind. It is easy to be sanctimonious about this when we ourselves are not challenged or affected, but a very different matter when our own wellbeing is at stake. For the solution lies with God and in Him alone can there be redemption. But God will not take the initiative without human involvement. To sit back and leave it all to God is not an option. God acts through His agents, who are spiritually aware human beings. We share the burden, which is not taken away from us, though we are given the support so that we may 'walk through the valley of the shadow of death, and fear no evil, for Thou art with me'. When we are truly inspired by God we lose our concern for self and become absorbed in our task, however vast it may be.

The dimension of social problems

How does the life of the spirit help in the battle against injustice and improper discrimination? It is necessary for us to be aware of current social trends and problems together with their underlying causes, so that we avoid the bigotry of the conservative thinker as well as the importunate zeal of the would-be reformer. The seeker after truth never loses a concern for the individual. Unfortunately we find it easier to rant against the injustices shown to others than to receive those down-and-out victims in person when they impinge upon our lives. This does not mean that we should calmly accept the unacceptable within government and society in general. But it does mean that our attitude should be to show compassion – to judge less and to love more.

The way of life

The quest of God does not demand that we retreat from the world.

Quite the contrary. We should be more than ever concerned with our fellows, with the animals in this planet and with the other creations on the earth and the universe which, if we destroy them, will lead to our own destruction. Yet the spiritually aware person is not a harbinger of gloom, but is aware of God's presence in all things. The spark of God within man ensures that human beings despite their own judgement usually manage to do the right thing in the end.

The key to successful living is moderation and balance in all things: the middle way of the Buddhist. This is the way to liberation, using the world's resources as we must but avoiding gluttony on the one hand and over-asceticism on the other. As we grow in spirituality we realise that our most important work is the task, locally, which lies before us. It is only by prayer that we may influence the larger world as a whole. The work is slow, but we have the Holy Spirit to guide us.

The psychic faculty and the spiritual path

As the personality becomes better integrated, the soul within it becomes more dominant. As we advance towards God, extra-sensory impressions may also enter our awareness. The materialist would dismiss all of this as imaginary, restricting all communication as restricted to the five senses. But as we become more aware of the silence around us, perceptions from within the field known as 'psychic' may become apparent to us. These communications are strictly personal in character. Some of them may be demonic in character, emanating from our own unconscious mind or from others around us. It is probable that some people with mental disorders have a heightened awareness of the psychic (whose source they cannot then determine), and some people take hallucinatory drugs to bring about such things. But the psychic realm is one of transition from the material to the eternal presence of the spiritual life and thus needs to be understood.

It is important to appreciate that the soul is the organ of both psychic information and spiritual enlightenment. The more active our reasoning mind or intellect, the more we exclude the psychic. On the other hand there are those who despite their intellect are open to the psychic and may pick up telepathic communication from those around them, and indeed even from those beyond the grave. If survival after death is important for us, we need to be open to the acquisition of the stillness which makes such things possible. In this sceptical age it may be helpful to remind ourselves that this psychic realm of communication that we dismiss is particularly open to the primitive races of the world who have not yet developed the reasoning part of their minds so as to exclude ubiquitous psychic impressions.

The intellect is a natural censor of our experiences. It tends to eliminate from the consciousness experiences that conflict with its logical picture of the world around it, not unlike the autonomic part of the brain that will re-educate itself following an injury to one of its organs such as hearing or eyesight. Thus the psychic is dismissed as 'impossible'. This dominance by the intellect is a feature of modern scientific society, and it is bitterly denounced by the various irrational groups that function in protest against the desiccating power of pure reason. Neither is correct. Whilst caution and discernment is necessary in examining the psychic, which can be false or misleading, a blanket denunciation of the psychic is a terrible error and can lead to excesses such as witch-burning which are both hideous and a denial of the whole truth.

But balance is indeed essential. Many of the evils of the past century, including Nazism, stem from a wholesale flight from reason into superstition and mass manipulation. Other occult groups of today fall into the same category.

The middle way which we are adjured to follow, calls for a courteous agnosticism. The materialists may scorn those emotional beings who claim to have entertained angels, and astronomers will amaze us with the nature of the material universe. Yet it is the mystics who will give us the meaning of reality. But even then do not take them on trust. Apply the test to each proposition: first the hypothesis, then the antithesis, proceeding to synthesis. 'By their fruits ye shall know them' is the acid test. Undeveloped psychic ability can be unattractive in the extreme and can boost the ego of the purveyor to the detriment of those around. It is a sad fact that so many spiritualist groups display such a low level of spirituality.

The gifts of the spirit

There is one attractive aspect to the psychic. The more one progresses on the spiritual path the more psychic one may become. This is usually far less spectacular than the spiritual gifts often displayed in Pentecostalism, but arguably of greater worth. The problem with overt spiritual gifts in emotional religious groups is that it tends to exalt the personality. The person so visited feels they have 'arrived' and are spiritually in a higher order than others less endowed. This of course invalidates the whole process. When psychic awareness develops as part of the integration of the personality, the outcome is far less obtrusive. It does not seek to make its presence obvious. It is more like the instinctive and positive relationship between two closely allied persons such as husband and wife – a mental telepathy that is wholesome. The proof lies in the confirmation of the spiritual matter on a worldly level. Sometimes the psychically aware person can perceive features of another person in the form of a radiance or 'aura' – said by some to be the origin of the halo ascribed to spiritually advanced souls.

Spiritual directors warn their disciples against the psychic path because in itself it can be but a dead end. To the extent that the occult at its lower orders conveys power or influence to the holder, it is of little worth and can be harmful. St Paul warns eloquently against such dangers by indicating that all such powers and gifts are worthless if they do not embrace love or charity. A psychic sense can be a useful adjunct to the personality but it is never infallible. Do not discard it, but do not rely totally upon it either. It may have its value in jolting some people out of a naive acceptance of mere humanism into a wider acceptance.

Why then does scientific investigation often seem to disprove the psychic? Partly because reason and cold prejudice subsume an open mind, even to the extent of defying reason, to the extent that whatever cannot be proved must therefore not exist.

Freedom and the will

An actively functioning mind is essential to the spiritual life. Yet this is often regarded with derision or mistrust. Religious people sometimes confuse the will with wilfulness. The spiritual person, it is said, must surely subjugate the personal will to the Will of God. If only it were that simple the advice might be sound! What is the Will of God? Often it is by no means clear for a variety of reasons. So we have to accept the existence of our own will as part of the fact of our lives. There is the will that arises from our practical experience of the world. There is also the will that stems from our unconscious minds, as taught by Freud and others. There is the will to survive, the will for sex, the will for power and the will for self-actualisation. And there is the inherited will from much religious observance which historically has often mixed fear of divine retribution with keenness to pursue the love of God.

Much of what passes for will in a successful person is in fact a series of responses to the challenges they may have faced since childhood. This does not mean that all successful people are immature. But Jesus asks, 'what shall it profit a man if he shall gain the whole world and lose his own soul?' Someone who is mainly driven by impulses is not really in control of themselves and lacks self-knowledge.

The freed will

Desire, though often decried in religious circles, often spurs us into action that is positive, especially if it promotes action for the good of others. At the lower levels there is the desire of the flesh which is mainly selfish. But in more evolved people there is a self-actualisation that promotes good and which leads us on to the spiritual path. Then the soul comes into its own and leads us to God. This leadership brings us freedom, especially when one has succeeded in doing the right thing in a crisis. Then one has learnt what true freedom of the will amounts to. One can act in accordance with the direction of the Spirit within and there is no need to placate or be subservient to others. We are then truly self-sufficient. Without being passive and waiting for God to do everything we can nonetheless 'be still and know that I am God'.

Contemplation is the most exalted activity that mankind can undertake.

Hence the end or purpose of the spiritual life is liberty. This is quite different from licence. It is a state of willed discipline to the highest level we know.

Discipline and the spiritual life

Discipline is needed to develop the spiritual life. Time needs to be set aside for worship and silent meditation. Exercise of the will is necessary. Having done this, then 'love God and do what you will'. These acts of will draw us closer to God, which is the aim – to worship God and enjoy Him forever, but as mature integrated human beings.

Mysticism and spirituality

There is an order of being that sustains life and draws it to its conclusion. It transcends material and personal life and is all-embracing. That is the experience of mysticism, which comes by the grace of God, for one never gets it wholly by striving for it. Mysticism comes more easily to those whose personality has become integrated. Those who indulge in drug-induced mysticism suffer disintegration, which is counter-productive. The characteristic 'high peak' of mysticism which practitioners recount involves awareness of a union with God and with all things. It is in the most sacred part of the soul, the spirit, that God reveals Himself to us. Time is devolved and eternity persists. Eternity is not an endless stream of time as a mathematician might define it, but a totality of being to which nothing, neither time nor space, can be added. Two essential elements are added in eternity: love and light. Love embraces all personality and embraces all creatures equally. The light of God is such that it illuminates all parts of creation.

Mystical illumination is such that it embraces the eternity of life and the forgiveness of sins. Forgiveness is unconditional stemming from the perfect love, and all that is required of us is the willingness to accept it. This leaves us free to pursue our path of integration. Guilt, revenge and other negative feelings can be left behind.

The hallmark of real mysticism is intuitive knowledge. It is the opening of the mind to a new understanding, termed gnosis. It speaks of the eternal order of things and of the ultimate realities. The mystic knows he or she is not of an 'elect'. What the mystic seeks to do is to radiate greater work, service, and healing to those round about.

The acceptance of God's forgiveness does not immediately make us perfect. This requires a long path of discipline involving a measure of what in the East is known as 'karma'. The path is straight and narrow, but not uphill. Its narrowness is a reflection of the Buddhist's middle way – the essential balance.

This unitive experience occurs as a milestone on the spiritual journey. It is not the end of the road. It comes like the wind, blowing where it will, which is the way of the Holy Spirit. No one is left without at least a fleeting glimpse of the infinite, though not everyone is accomplished enough to realise the full heights. Once again, the acid test is 'by their fruits ye shall know them'. Many people try to force the pace of spirituality by artificial means, and this does not bear fruit. Those with various forms of mental illness may experience unsound manifestations of mysticism, but mysticism is most convincing in healthy, balanced people whose work in the world is creative and self-effacing. It is inner balance that distinguishes the real mystic from the mentally unbalanced person.

If the modern mystic is to be compared with previous mystics from earlier times, the difference will lie in their attitude to the world. Inordinate self-denial is no longer seen as essential, and modern psychology contributes to our understanding of humanity, not all of which is conducive to religion. Mysticism is not only compatible with a healthy and balanced social life but essential if the mystic is to play a full part in everyday affairs. The spiritual person must be informed about current affairs. The world will never be the same as it was before Karl Marx, and in no way should we withdraw into a religious by-way, though we may temporarily retreat in order to recollect ourselves. Deprived people can never achieve full self-actualisation. St Paul reminds us that we are all members one of another. The summons to life leads us from self-centredness to an awareness of God, but we ourselves have to discover the path.

Discerning the spiritual path

Spiritual advancement is evidenced by the altered character of the aspirant, who radiates a light that illumines those around us. To have the kingdom of heaven we must lose self-concern in our involvement for others, whilst acknowledging that whatever we do is going to be inadequate and accepting this fact.

Those endowed with great temporal power or influence seldom achieve deep spiritual insight. An unnoticed servant may exhibit remarkable spirituality. We need to remember St Paul's definitions of the gifts or fruits of spirituality: love, joy, long-suffering, gentleness, goodness, faith, meekness and temperance. There is one more that might be added: a sense of humour, which is really an extension of balance that is linked with temperance.

The antithesis of balance is an inordinate intensity of purpose. Over-dogmatic missionaries can fall into this trap. They become so convinced of their own vocation that they feel they have to act as God's deputy. The same can apply to those of us who become over-absorbed in other causes such as social or animal welfare, sexual morality, racial or gender issues. Intensity of purpose can override a concern for people, and make obsessional cranks of us all. Spiritual people change the world by spontaneous reaction and not by denunciations. Reconciliation is the answer, and this is not the same as resignation or weakness. We must have unconditional love for all the parties in a dispute.

St Paul's 'gifts of the spirit' are often sought and valued by those seeking the spiritual life, and they can be more exciting than the fruits of the spirit listed above as though they were of greater value and more difficult to obtain. But though more spectacular they can be obtained independently of spirituality. The true spiritual master is to be identified by his or her obvious goodness and love.

But unspiritual people may acquire or possess psychic gifts. Not all spiritual healers are themselves spiritual and the closer one gets to the divine source, the less important psychic gifts become, though they cannot be denied and they have their uses.

Of techniques

The ascent of the mind to God cannot be achieved solely by the personal will. The grace of God is needful, though it can operate more readily with a prepared personality. Not all 'preparations' are sound however. The use of drugs has manifest weaknesses, and it can lead to greater self-centredness, which is clearly counter-productive. Eastern meditation techniques have their value, though they can result in a loss of personal identity that has led to objections from those qualified in psychiatry. Be that as it may, it is important to identify those personalities who ought to avoid meditation. Established Christians tend to benefit greatly from meditation since they often have the inner strength and balance that is needed. Used to outward action in their faith, a quiet contemplation can offer a valuable counter-balance.

Spiritual experience is but a small part of the spiritual life. There are no short cuts, and we have to be resilient in meeting the troughs as well as the peaks of daily life; so a technique needs not to become an end in itself. Similarly caution needs to be exercised in assessing certain aspects of the charismatic movement, which can open the person to psychic undercurrents, not all of which are helpful. Gifts, such as 'speaking with tongues', are not to be decried as neurotic manifestations (as its critics sometimes maintain), but neither are they the ultimate in prayer. They are liberating experiences in themselves provided the psychic energy so released does not do harm in unbalanced people. The same caution applies to all the wonderful experiences described in the Acts of the Apostles. The personality must be sufficiently balanced to handle them.

Yoga on the other hand can be of greater value in the spiritual ascent. Both the body and the will are placed in balance, as well as the mind. The problem with Eastern methods is the inadequate attention placed upon Divine Grace, because the personal nature of God is not emphasised as with Western Faiths. What is needed is a synthesis of both East and West as is now practised in some Catholic quarters. There are of course established techniques such as the Ignatian spiritual exercises, not all of which find wide acceptance outside their own religious orders or environments.

Each of us must find techniques which suit ourselves, and for this reason we should not decry other methods that may suit others.

Of teachers

Guidance on the spiritual path is of the greatest importance. Some people have advanced knowledge and this they should share. Teaching in yoga and meditation is especially important. Not all psychic gifts are harmful, but an ability to discern which spirits are helpful and which harmful is especially important, as well as an understanding of modern psychology. A genuine teacher is humble and unobtrusive, and does not overwhelm others. A teacher should not be approached from afar. There is an Eastern proverb 'when the pupil is ready the master appears'. The appearance may be casual, but the impact quite clear. A special kind of teacher is the guru, but this is not for everyone. The danger of over-adherence to one source of wisdom is the risk of fundamentalism. This becomes the only source and therefore everything else must be wrong. This does not work, for the truth has to be lived and discovered by each of us for ourselves.

Of communities

Religious communities flourish within several faith groups, notably the Catholic Church and Buddhism. The community life is not a soft option, and is not for all. Life is a constant relationship, and all real living is meeting, as Buber puts it. Many non-religious groups try to work together but fall apart, lacking the love of God. It is possible to imagine groups who form together with God's love, and indeed these may form the churches of the future.

The spiritual path

The spiritual path embraces the whole of life. The fruitful life should also be an active life in the world. For the fruit of the spiritual life is joy. The troubles of this life are nothing compared to the joy that is to come. In interpreting the mystical life nothing is more important than a balance between intuition and intellect. We should take every chance of broadening our horizons so that a beatific experience to ourselves can the more effectively be represented to others.

Building the spiritual body

The ultimate purpose of our life on earth is to build such a spiritual reality that will continue after our earthly body is cast off. There is only one existence, which is eternal life. If we persist in faith we find that death is the gateway to life. What is the most important thing we have to gain in our earthly life? Not wealth, nor power, nor prestige, nor intellectual knowledge, nor pleasure. The one thing that survives is love.

We begin to prepare for death as soon as we are born. Age can help us as with experience we grow closer to truth. Our great work is the forging of relationships. Love is a deep care for others, not just that which is promoted by mutual self-interest.

The event of earthly death is awesome. There is no absolute proof of survival, although a good deal of persuasive evidence from spiritualists and others exists. Ultimately our survival at death is a personal experience. Yet in going on alone we realise that we are not truly alone, but supported by unseen hosts including the souls of our earthly friends. This can be brought about by intercessory prayer, including communion with those who have gone ahead of us. We stand naked and alone at the point of death, but at this moment spiritual reality succeeds mortal life. We then receive a new light – the light of love. And this may come from the full communion of saints, depending to some extent on how we have lived on earth. 'Make unto yourself friends of the mammon of unrighteousness' as in the parable of Luke 16.9. and they will receive us. In the greater world no secrets can be hidden.

In this relationship we can see the pattern of heaven and hell. We are in hell when we are immersed in ourselves and our problems. Such hell is bad enough on earth but it can be a good deal worse in the afterlife if we have not managed to free ourselves from it. Indeed it is suggested that some people in that state do not even realise that they have died. But there is no question of punishment by God or by any other power. Indeed the forces of light and love are constraining to break through to us if only we can receive them; working towards our ultimate redemption.

The soul and the spiritual body

What survives physical death? To the atheist and the humanist the answer has to be 'nothing'. But to those of us who have lived the spiritual life there is the duality of mind or soul and body, though this is decried by materialists of all kinds. And when the task of the body is complete the combination of mind and soul, the spirit, is released into a larger existence that is beyond time and space. Spiritualistic communication taps the superficial mental capacity of the deceased through a medium and the material thus released can often be trivial and seldom progressive. At the level of the soul however there can be direct communion between lover and loved. The problem of mediumistic communication is that much of it can be open to doubt. For this reason one can seldom be enthusiastic about it, even though it may bring comfort to the bereaved because of the evidence of survival.

It is said that the post-mortem existence is so different from that on earth that no one who has died could effectively describe it to us, which is true, though our earthly personalities do not immediately cease, and we may spend some time re-living our earthly experiences, 'as we sow so shall we reap'. But in essence we are our own judges when we can perceive the results of our actions.

There is the Christian's hope that after death we shall meet Christ face to face. In one sense this may be too naive to be wholly true, yet in the after-life we certainly become more aware of the cosmic dimensions of the Christ, as we progress from an immediate 'hell' or 'purgatory' to a 'paradise' or 'heaven' or 'summerland'. This can be subject to debate but my own experience has satisfied me that the newly deceased learn things too wonderful for us to fathom, and it may also be likened to the post-discussion after an examination. What went well and what went badly, for we all pass and fail in some respects.

Yet the ultimate kind of 'heaven' of eternal bliss or passive 'Nirvana' that is promised to the conservative orthodox religionist would arguably be a kind of hell if it were true. And which advanced soul would choose Nirvana for him or herself while so much suffering existed in material creation? The forgiveness of Christ allows us to continue our path of service and rebirth unhampered by the burden of our transgressions.

Reincarnation

The term 'rebirth' immediately raises the question of reincarnation. How large and diverse the universe may be is not known and it would be presumptuous to assume that what we can perceive is the only theatre in which the soul can exist and serve God. However it seems likely that many souls do assume a human body on more than one occasion. Reports of psychic workers with young children displaying pre-natal memories is arguably more convincing than the memories of adults who may display what is termed 'crypt-amnesia'.

A snare in discussing rebirth or reincarnation is the suggestion that guilt or 'karma' can progress from one life to another so that misfortune today is a 'payback' from earlier life. But in Christ we go beyond this and live by love. At all events the soul grows through experience, and the rule is 'do to others as you would have them do to you'. Some grandiose accounts of rebirth attribute all a person's misfortunes to the sins of earlier lives, and this is not impressive. 'Greater love has no man than this, that he give his life for his friend' (St John 15.13) enables us to rise above the trivialities of what rebirth does or does not achieve.

Survival of the spiritual body

The foregoing is a personal expression of faith and as such is founded on experience. The readers, however, must themselves judge and discriminate.

There is no scientific proof of survival after death. This is because there is no total proof of identity. If you send me a message post-mortem, how do I know it's from you? Direct communication can only be telepathic, and not everyone can achieve this, even in life. Once you introduce a medium, to what extent does a third party now intervene and influence the message? True communion with the deceased is a spiritual act. In the parable of Dives and Lazarus the rich man is told that if the living will not heed the prophets, neither will they respond even if one were to rise from the dead'. (Luke 16. 19-31). A generation seeking after signs will merely explain each sign away and carry on as before. The history of spiritualism and psychic research bears this out.

Christ, after His crucifixion, only appeared to those who were His friends. He did not appear to those who had persecuted Him even though such an appearance may have influenced them. Christ's way is the way of freedom, not coercion. Thus those who have had the veil between heaven and earth dissolved for them will accept the fact of survival and the meaning of immortality.

Immortality and resurrection

The soul is the permanent factor in our existence. The body is cast off at death, though aspects of the emotion and personality may subsist for some time, and may even emerge in the form of memories of past lives, as previously discussed. The soul is the essential life. It is unique and it is in communion with all other souls, and this forms the matrix of the created universe.

The concept of soul is of course beyond the range of ordinary reason. It continues in time until all is united in God. An evil soul that causes mass destruction and misery might forfeit its identity. But I look to the love of God and the final redemption of all creation, as foreshadowed by the mystics through the ages. This is the meaning of immortality.

The resurrection of the body is the reverse side of the immortality of the soul. It is not to be thought of as a crude raising of the physical body, long decayed, at the 'last day' so that it can come together. It is to be understood as the raising into a new life of spiritual vibrancy. There is at least an intellectual and emotional resurrection.

We live to give ourselves unreservedly to the redemption of the world. It is asked, 'How could one saint remain in heaven as long as there is one sinner left in hell?' which may sum up the reality. Nothing, however evil, is beyond the redeeming power of God. At the end we shall love our neighbour as ourself, realising that we are indeed our neighbour.

If we can live spiritually now we can accept the summons to eternal life. And when the night comes and we can do no further work, the Light of God will illuminate us into new realms of exploration.

5. Precarious Living - The Path to Life

This book opens with a vision. The author is descending down a constantly spiral staircase toward a pit of darkness. There is a funereal procession of wraithlike other souls collecting at the bottom, orderly but in a kind of disorder. Fear and resentment well up, for he does not want to leave the world thus. Then a wisp of fresh air blows and a voice says *'I am the way, I am the truth and I am the life; no one comes to the Father except by me'*. The author goes his way in peace and thanksgiving.

This, the second book that Martin Israel wrote, contains within 'One Man's Path' a good deal of autobiographical material which has been outlined elsewhere in the present volume and will therefore not be repeated save in outline. He had been urged to include this personal testimony by a friend who felt it would be helpful for the reader to know something of the background to his life and inspiration. Wisdom, Martin feels, comes primarily from our own experience, and this is the way to authentic life.

The Call

There is a call that leads us to higher fulfilment in our lives, which we may ignore if we wish, but which enables us to embrace a life of deeper significance. It may come to us at a time of deep distress, or else upon witnessing some deed of self-sacrifice, or maybe on seeing a noble work of art. It may or may not have strong religious overtones, perhaps from the voice of a preacher. Whatever the means, our call brings a light that illuminates the deepest part of our being, the soul; and it leads us to eternity.

The Light on the Path

The path onto which we are led leads us also towards a knowledge of God. In travelling this path we soon realise we live in two worlds – the spiritual and the secular. These two worlds have to be actively confronted and integrated if we are not to fall apart in our quest. We have to realise that all people are members one of another and that no one who is a full human being can isolate themselves from injustice wherever it may occur. Yet it is the way we learn to deal with this injustice that separates the spiritual person from the mere rabble-rouser who pursues justice primarily for their own ends.

Illumination

The mystical life is divided into three stages: purgation, illumination and union. This is an over-simplification since the purging goes on until eternal union has been achieved, and in this world there was only one person who fully achieved union with God, and that was Jesus Christ. Purgation involves suffering. Suffering brings redemption which enables us to become more aware of God's love and light and thus allows us to progress. To some of us, however, there comes a specific instance of beatific illumination that forms a landmark in our lives and a foundation for our future development.

The power and love of God is bestowed equally on all creatures. No particular group or sect is favoured, and it comes to us all when we are ready to receive it. There is no wrath of God, but only wrath in the disregarded law that brings about suffering as an inevitable result. Yet the final end of pain is joy and redemption.

Progress in our lives, as in Martin's own life, may involve 'the dark night of the soul' which has to be lived through, and may be followed by a dawning of the light. In a section called 'A Return to the Roots' various denominations, teachings and creeds are evaluated.

The Language of the Path

Perhaps the most helpful concept of human nature is Plato's division into body, soul and spirit, used to such effect by St Paul. To this may be added the mind.

The mind is the part of us which reacts to inner sensations and outer circumstances arising from the body. This reaction reveals itself in feeling, thinking and willing a given action. It is sometimes called the 'psyche'. The central part of our conscious mind is the self, closely allied to the 'ego' of Freudian teaching. But the range of the mind is much greater than this, encompassing ideas, impulses, thoughts and feelings which we can observe and judge if we wish. And beneath this are many more powerful urges of the subconscious mind that we cannot observe. This is the field of the psychoanalyst who may assess our motives and impulses. They are however not completely submerged, for they may be released in sleep, possibly taking upon themselves symbolic characteristics within dreams.

Within different levels of our subconscious mind are those animal instincts with which we are born, some of them dark; and those parental guidance 'dos' and 'don'ts' instilled by family and by society as we grow. There is also a level at which our higher aspirations are represented, be they artistic, inventive or ethical. If these different levels are not in balance but one or the other dominates, we become emotionally crippled and cannot become full people. St Paul in the seventh chapter of Romans identifies this conflict in the mind. 'For the good that I would, I do not; but the evil that I would not, that I do'. Only God through Jesus Christ can ultimately resolve this conflict. And in the painful process of getting to know ourselves we realise we are not as the world sees us, nor even as we like to see ourselves. But the radiance of self-knowledge is the true aim of the mystic, whose soul reaches full development in its ability to give itself in love to others.

In the very centre of the soul is the 'spark', the highest and holiest part. This is the spirit, or what the Quakers call the part of God that is in man. This is the part in each one of us that allows us to dare to develop into fully adjusted people. We then live for others, not so much by self-denial as by showing a real concern for others – including ourselves.

Becoming a person means becoming an integrated individual in whom body, mind and soul are working together under the guidance of the spirit. Few of us achieve this. A person is not perfect. Only the spirit is perfect, for that is our image of God. Most of us are a long way from knowing our spirit, and hence are incomplete persons.

Do we really have free will? Or is our path predetermined? Religion has it that we are free to choose our way of life. The extreme behavioural psychologist, however, will have it that we are mainly governed by stimuli. Psychology has taught us a lot, but there is more to humanity than Pavlovian response. This does not mean that our will cannot become enslaved. An enslaved will ensures that our whole life may become devoted to acquiring money, power, influence, fame, to the exclusion of all else and we may develop an iron will in the pursuit and so may succeed. But beneath the facade there may be the frightened child terrified of failure and bereft should we fail. This is not freedom.

Alternatively we may be driven by passive impulses – by a conscience, that in the proverb 'makes cowards of us all', though it propels us to heights of good work or charity. Psychologically this probably arises from conditioning and environment as well as a wish to plumb a deeper awareness of our true nature. In such a case the 'right' path is that which contributes to true self-development. Over-anxiety with apparent results can be self-defeating. When we can detach ourselves from the conditioning that is propelling us then can we progress. 'Holy Indifference' is a term used to describe the saints.

Total freewill is seldom achieved because of the conditions that surround us. The will can either be enslaved by impulses or else it can aspire to greater things, the service of God, by pursuing the highest it knows. Then can the words of the Collect for Peace be realised, 'O God, whose service is perfect freedom ...'

But what of predestination? We may have freewill but can we control our destiny? There is a power far above us that knows even when a sparrow falls to the ground. Those with the psychic powers of prediction or precognition are very much aware of the extent to which affairs may be pre-ordained. But two things are clear. We may choose our own path and may succeed or fail. And if we fail, there is later a chance to make amends and to achieve redemption.

We have a will that we can use, to leave behind the animal drives that may hold us back. By prayer and by the guidance of the Holy Spirit we may be helped, which leads us towards love. It has been said, 'Love and do what you will'. With true love our motives are pure.

The range of the mind is vast, the greater part of it being subconscious. It includes what Jung called the 'collective unconscious'. This is in touch with the soul of the rest of the universe, and it is in this sense that St Paul tells us that we are each members one of another. If we were living fully in the Spirit, we would also be conscious of this.

Because of this interconnection it might be expected that from time to time flashes of extra-sensory perception might occur. And so indeed they do, especially in the primitive races of the world where the brain acts less as a filter - not being preoccupied with the affairs of existence in a materialist and scientific modern environment. For as we grow in intelligence so our minds tend to separate us from the collective unconscious. We have to pass through this phase to a greater level of self-actualisation before we break through this separation and realise our corporate as well as our individual identity. This enables us to be self-giving, which is an essential in our path to God.

We may experience the psychical, which is personal to us and comes to us from the lower parts of our subconscious, and the spiritual which is transpersonal or universal and appertains to the spark or the spirit. Some aspects of the lower part of our subconscious may become demonic, especially if our conscious will is seriously frustrated. Unless this frustration is faced and dealt with positively it can result in a corruption which in the worst case can spread into the corporate life and lead to such communal evils as Nazism. This is part of the precariousness of our present life. Should these evil corrupt influences spread into the next life, and it is probable that they can and do, then they can give rise to the kind of possession of weak willed humans in this life that is sometimes called 'demonic'.

Other far less dangerous examples of the psychic include clairvoyance, premonitions, the sensing of 'atmospheres' in places where horrendous things have happened. More positively some gifted people can sense positive atmospheres, for example in country churches where prayer has been felt for many years. And there may be favourable instances of positive messages coming from mediums or sensitives conveying messages of a spiritual kind, though one would hesitate to describe them as spiritual in essence. True saintliness does not come by these means. At most they can help, but spiritual directors of all faiths advise their adherents not to become trapped in the apparent glamour of psychic phenomena and communication.

The highest spiritual communication comes from God to our spirit. It transcends all other communication and leads us to total reality.

'What does it profit a man if he gain the whole world and lose his own soul?' asks Jesus. Whatever leads us away from a preoccupation with ourselves to a fuller participation in the world and in the affairs of other people leads us towards God. This is summarised in Jesus' two great commandments 'Love God' and 'Love your neighbour as yourself.' Whenever someone says or does something that raises our spirits, it is as if it comes from God.

Whereas the psychical impinges on all aspects of our psyche, it only becomes spiritual when it tells of God – and thus becomes mystical. Other kinds of psychic communication speak to the isolated soul and do not decrease its isolation. Moreover they may be positive or negative. For this reason such communications are hazardous and should not be initiated from the living to the dead. This is an area of activity that should only be undertaken by trained and dedicated workers.

Survival after death has never been scientifically proved because even the most convincing communication from our deceased loved ones can be ascribed to mechanisms that do not require there to be a post mortem existence. This is particularly true of mediumistic communication where there are ample instances of material emanating from the medium's own mind. However when all of the evidence from the various instances of communication is assessed a very good case can be made for survival after death. But each of us must make up our own minds.

If as I believe there is indeed survival after death, then it is the psyche which survives. And the psyche of a newly deceased person may not be very different from the condition it was in when alive. We may even experience in our more vivid dreams the same kind of environment that awaits us immediately after our death.

It has been said that we make our old age in our youth. A selfish young person tends to become crabbed in old age, whereas a dedicated person will develop into a blessed and loved old person. It is my view that the darkness that surrounds the self-centred old man or woman will pass with them into the next life, whereas the radiance and love that surrounds the good human being will likewise pass over with them. This is the meaning of hell and heaven. However the immediate post mortem state is not the final one. I have no doubt that if the deceased wicked person can face their wickedness and repent, then an opportunity is still open to them to rise from hell to heaven. To those who complain that such a view is not biblical, two points should be made. The first is that such a post mortem progression is extremely painful and tortuous. It is difficult enough to face one's sins on earth where one can hide within one's body. After death, when you have no body, you are completely open to 'the whole company of heaven' and you are your own judge as well. The second point is that eternal punishment is incompatible with the love of God, and our sins exist in eternity – they cannot be undone – and in that sense no redemption is possible.

It is unfortunate that scriptures often seem to depict a vengeful God, but this represents a human view of crime and punishment. The real punishment for the sinner is separation from the love of God. It is the sinner who does the separating and who must make the first move. And what we have done wrong has then to be restored, for our own sake as well as for our victims. Restitution comes as part of forgiveness. Forgiveness opens the way for us to continue working for the good of those we have harmed, unhampered by guilt but motivated by love. When we are forgiven and motivated by love and not by selfishness then we can advance towards becoming full persons.

The concept of a spiritual body or extensive psyche, not enclosed within a physical body, is hard for us to envisage in this life. St Paul discusses this in depth in Chapter 15 of 1 Corinthians, the passage that culminates in the verse, 'O death, where is thy sting. O grave, where is thy victory?' Esoteric writers describe a series of 'bodies' that we have: a subtle body, an astral body, a spiritual body. This is an area of study in itself, derived partly from Hindu metaphysics and open to some who have clairvoyant gifts. The body that we shall have in the next life is more glorious than our earthly body because we are closer to Christ, and as St Paul also describes, the universe itself is to be freed from the shackles of mortality and will enter into the liberty and splendour of the children of God (Romans 8:21).

It is clear that no one on earth in one life can achieve the perfection attained by Jesus Christ. Hence the immediate life after death needs to provide an opportunity for further development. The Catholic concept of Purgatory, a state between heaven and hell in which the soul can be further purified, seems to be the correct one. It is correct, provided it is extended to include those of all faiths who aspire to seek God in love. It seems realistic, however, that some will go through a physical rebirth or reincarnation, as Eastern religion teaches.

Eternal life is of another order from all of this, and yet it interrelates with all of these states. Eternity is a state of ultimate reality. It is known to the mystic in a brief glimpse. It is the ultimate state or goal of mankind. It is a new kind of existence outside time and space where in St Paul's words, 'I live, yet not I, but Christ liveth in me.' To the Buddhist it is Nirvana. Against it, all other modes of existence pale into insignificance.

Milestones on the Path

The path of life is the one that leads away from illusions to reality, towards knowing oneself. Travelling this path can be daunting because it involves breaking away from what is conventionally 'right' and following the path to self awareness. It involves experiencing life itself, and this can be better than the various psychological techniques and meditations. Self awareness involves facing oneself as one really is; especially when under stress or anxiety. Anyone can behave well when they are feeling good. But it is by facing the darkness that is within us all that we are able to progress. If we persevere we will see that we are even now in a form of eternal life.

It is a well-known discipline of those pursuing a spiritual life that each night they should recollect what they have done during the day and reflect upon it. This is arguably better than the kind of technique which involves pausing to think each time during the day before we do anything. We need a measure of spontaneity. The one worthwhile goal in life is that we should each become an authentic person, and full of the Spirit of God in fellowship with others.

How often do we, in early life, adopt the style of another person that we respect and seek to model ourselves upon them? Eventually our own persona asserts itself, and this facade is broken. There are two approaches. One involves following a prescribed path or formula such as a religious vocation. The other involves following an inner impulse that may be less comfortable because it is less secure. But in each case there needs to be a true calling from the Holy Spirit otherwise there is a risk that one will 'gain the whole world and lose one's own soul'.

The way of self-awareness involves being attuned to the Holy Spirit. This leads us into all truth. We have to perceive ourselves as we really are. We have to acknowledge ourselves, including the darkness, and offer it in prayer, accepting the truth as it is and not maybe as we might wish it. 'O Lord I thank thee that I am not as others are' is the trap into which the postulant can fall, whereas the only possible stance is 'Have mercy on me a sinner'. This disperses pride – the deadliest of sins – and allows true self-acceptance.

The paradox is that as soon as we have achieved self-acceptance we should let it go. It gives us self-love sufficient to love our neighbours as ourselves, but then we must move from self-concern to concern for others, without which we fall back on ourselves.

When we dream our conscious mind becomes dormant and the unconscious takes over. It is known to be an integral part of sleep, but some people dream a lot and others hardly at all. We can be closer to truth when we dream. Some dreams come to us in symbols. There is more than one way of interpreting dreams, which tells us that the only true way is that which comes from the dreamer themselves. Dreams that relate to past or present events can tell us how our conscious and unconscious minds are related at this point, and may give us a guide as to our behaviour. The subject is interesting and relevant, and suitable for deep study if it does not assume an overwhelming importance in our lives. There may be a psychic element in dreams which itself can be valuable. Dreams as such should be distinguished from visions, which are revelations coming to us when we are fully awake. Both dreams and visions are dramatic manifestations that can show us something about our relations with creation and with God.

We suffer when our personalities are not aligned with God. Suffering began when freewill began because this allowed separation from God. It is ever-present as long as we are free. Our freedom is a measure of God's love, since the alternative would be that we were mere ciphers. The way of suffering is hard and unremitting; its aim is to remove whatever separates us from God. We suffer not only because we are out of alignment but also because the world is out of alignment. Suffering that opens the heart of the victim, allows them freedom from self-pity and admission into a sphere of understanding. Everyone on the road to salvation has to experience suffering. It is a part of growing into a full person.

What of those who have 'lost their faith' and see no point in persevering? Sometimes this arises from the staleness of a cut and dried orthodox religious upbringing where all is black or white. Today there are many alternative manifestations of the Holy Spirit, which blows where it will, and they should be open to such avenues of faith.

Pride is of course the cardinal sin, since the others tend to stem from it. But it should be separated from self-esteem, which is not a sin at all but a necessary state for us to be able to progress.

What is there to be said about cosmic disasters? How and why do they arise? This is a deep question to which no clear answer exists. The extent to which malign human or diabolic forces can intervene is unclear. St Paul describes a world liberated from all this into which the children of God will one day be admitted.

No one has ever encountered God directly because no one, other than the Son of God made flesh, could survive the encounter. Some people who expound their belief in God in terms which suggest they understand or 'know' Him are sometimes worshipping a construct of their own making. Those who are gaining in spiritual awareness tend to be much less certain or dogmatic about the nature of God. To be less certain about God is not a sign of unbelief but of a degree of humility that is a prerequisite. As we develop our faith deepens but we cease to see God in an exclusive, personal way. The world's great mystics affirm the unknowability of God. Yet paradoxically the quiet unassuming mind can be receptive to the grace of God. We can then receive God within the personal pronoun 'He' although the masculinity implied within this term is unfortunate and not really appropriate, especially when contemplating the Three Persons of the Trinity. To receive knowledge of God we have to be quiet and humble. To achieve this we need to practise meditation. There is now a plethora of information about meditation, and the author briefly summarises his own opinions as to what it should entail.

Meditation is no panacea. It does not remove physical or psychological or even moral impediments. It is possible, for example, that a seasoned criminal might become a more effective criminal if he were to meditate. However for the most part it is a health-giving mental activity that can lead to spiritual renewal and a better prayer life. It can help our personalities to achieve balance. Meditation can give us peace and the kind of peace that Jesus gave to those who would receive it. When we have this peace we ourselves can give it to the world. Meditation enables us to develop human relationships. When we can hear another's life story without feeling the urge to intervene with our own wisdom, we are approaching the point where we can produce a greater wisdom, the wisdom of God. This will be for the benefit of ourselves as well as for the person to whom we speak.

Prayer begins when the heart is open in compassion to the world around, and into the wider life of the communion of saints. Prayer is a venture in faith that has validity if we believe in a greater being that comes to us in love. Meditation on the other hand stills the mind so that we can be open to God but there is no commitment. Prayer is a meeting in which we present ourselves as 'a whole and living sacrifice' in the words of St Paul. There is only one thing that we can in some measure give to God, and that is the love that He first gave to us, and it comes from us renewed and vibrant. The prime initiator of prayer is the Holy Spirit that is within us. It seems to some that the confession of sin that is part of the Christian prayer can become exaggerated, but those on the spiritual path know better. We are all the time balanced precariously between self-indulgence and selflessness. Often the indulgence wins in the first instance, but the Spirit then wins the ultimate battle before undue harm is done. Once we can face our sin, both as an overall attitude and in specific actions then we can offer it to God. His love will forgive us and we can begin the process of redemption. The essential fruit of prayer is not to have our petitions answered but an opening out of ourselves so that we can see around us in compassion and love. At its heart is silent communion with God. Enunciated prayers from the liturgy serve to quieten our minds and are helpful. But the ultimate is to 'be still and know that I am God.' The purpose is for our souls to communicate with God. When we are least aware of ourselves this communion takes place. It is the elevation of our minds to God. Petition and intercession, though valuable and never to be despised, are in the foothills of prayer. There is only one petition worth making and that is that God's will be done, through us, if appropriate.

That supreme institution the Lord's Prayer has many petitionary elements including that one. But it should not be assumed that the cosmic nature of things is going to be changed by our prayer. It is rather that our own consciousness and integrity may be altered so that things otherwise beyond us become within our grasp. For if we ask in silence, the Holy Spirit will infuse us with new life so that we can do the work more efficiently ourselves and with finer results. God does not do the work for us.

Thus prayers for earthly powers and wealth are vain. They may come about, but not necessarily for our good. Remember the greatest of prayers 'Let this cup pass from me, but not as I wilt but as thou will.'

So what of prayers about cosmic disasters? The rationalist will query prayers against flood, tempest and 'acts of God'. Yet in dire straits we turn to prayer, and are often ready to forget our prejudices when all seems lost and 'there is none other that fighteth for us but only Thou, O Lord.' And there is evidence that group prayer works. How it works is not clear but I have no doubt that this prayer is proper, possibly influencing the cosmos in ways unknown to us.

Service to others is the way to know God. Neither the deepest prayer nor the most effective meditation are of significance until they have been fertilised by service. Service must be accompanied by love. If we serve with a cold resentful heart it can be as if we are cursing the other person. 'To give and not to count the cost, nor to seek any reward save that of knowing that we do the will of God' is the hallmark of true service. But service does bring its own reward, often helping us to recover after some trauma or bereavement. Life in the world is a continuous and arduous process of self giving and service. This is the way of love.

God alone can define the depths of love. To love another involves passing through the phase where we tend to ascribe to them all the attributes we think we possess ourselves, to the stage of recognising them as an independent being with their own characteristics, some of which we may not like or agree with. This is the test of love. Love proves itself in service, and that service continues through all manner of vicissitudes. If we cannot face this truth we cannot grow as a full person. Tragically some people go through life not facing this, even though they may be devout religionists, but that kind of religion avails them nothing. True love enables the lover to love more widely and less exclusively. It avoids the kind of obsessive or possessive love that can ruin some marriages. This is tolerance, in the deeper meaning.

Love is warm and ardent, though on occasion it has to be cold and forbidding. It is right to show displeasure when the other person is behaving wrongly or selfishly. This may be a more meaningful loving response than a cold but convenient acceptance. But the other person should never be forsaken. With love there is a time when forgiveness should prevail over personal resentment and anger, however. There is a spark of divinity in all of us and there can be times when a loving act can trigger this spark in another. This operates when God is involved. If we try and do it on our own we run the risk of becoming inflated with our own importance and 'good works', which is the mark of the Pharisee in the parable. In the story of Martha and Mary there is a tendency for readers to assume that Jesus is rating contemplation as a higher virtue than good works. But this is a mistake. What is being taught here is that the problem lies in the resentment in Martha that her sister is not helping her. Were she correctly oriented she could have been part of her sister's happiness, and content in the contribution she was making. The basis of service is that it is done to the glory of God. In George Herbert's words, 'Who sweeps a room as for thy sake, makes that and the action fine!'

A sacrament is defined as an outward and visible sign of an inward and spiritual grace. In the Christian Church it is confined to Baptism, the Eucharist and certain other liturgical acts. But life itself is a sacrament. Through taking part in life's trials we are gaining essential knowledge. We learn not from eminent teachers but from the events in our daily lives and our response to them. If we seek outer reward for what we do we misunderstand the purpose of these events. But if we give of ourselves unstintingly we shall emerge at least to some extent in touch with eternal values.

In the Eucharist there is a mystery that defies rational explanation. It is an 'image' of Christ's death and passion, which is too vast to explain. But one thing is clear. The bread and wine do undergo a change in their spiritual nature when they are consecrated by one who is dedicated to a priestly office. While never ceasing to be their original earthly substance, they are now exalted to be a part of the body and blood of Christ. Whatever is consecrated to God's service is redeemed and becomes holy, yet it never ceases to be itself. There is no merging. But there is a union. In the Transfiguration when Jesus was shown to the disciples in the form of Universal God, He was nonetheless still also Himself in the earthly form. This needs to be understood. A potential error is the one that sees God in all things, and nothing apart from God. Yet this denies the individual existence of that which is created. The correct relationship is that of identity-in-difference. We are neither identical nor totally separate. In the Eucharist, mankind grows a little closer to the Divine, which alas is still hidden from us.

Our everyday life is a sacrament. In this, true religion helps us with our approach to Divine reality, whereas false religion impedes us. If we are helped, our work is no longer a burden. The world is never quite the same after even the lowliest of us has performed some task however menial with love and dedication. As we become more aware of this, we may find ourselves less concerned with overtly religious sacraments, turning more towards a Quakerly view, such as the sacrament of silence, though this is not necessary.

The Sacrament of the Present Moment is a term introduced by the 18th century Jesuit Jean-Pierre de Caussade. Every situation brings us closer to the divine grace if we are willing to receive it. To reach this sacrament all the other disciplines need also to be mustered in order to fill our lives and to bring us in effect from death into life. Many blessings accrue when we live life sacramentally. The person who loves life has already passed from death into the life eternal. We become less concerned about the future. We may hope for success but we are more willing to leave the outcome to God. It brings about the kind of positive thinking that is sound, and not merely a 'feel-good' mechanism. It cultivates the 'holy indifference' that can be a guard against active negative thinking, which can certainly do harm in psychic as well as other fields. Despair can be infectious and needs to be avoided. The antidote is to go into a quiet place, away from those who keep talking negatively, and pray.

We do not live alone. Our existence is built on relationships. And each relationship is sacred. This is especially so in the marriage relationship and in the act of sexual union, whose primary purpose is spiritual if correctly oriented. The other purposes including procreation are arguably secondary. Today we have fallen far in our society from recognising these truths. There is a Christhood in store for all of us that we shall pass from corruption to eternity and spiritual reality.

There are, however, some warnings on the way. God is present with us on our journey and does not have to be sought. The unselfconscious child within us, however, can relate to this more easily than the seasoned adult. 'Unless ye become as little children...' The developed mind tends to kill imaginations and so dull our senses to aspects of the spiritual. We need to develop knowledge which is not harmful, provided it does not become an end in itself. And temperate living aids the spiritual quest whereas physical indulgence hinders it. Meditation can be an aid, as also can the Hindu practice of Yoga.

The dedicated person will never be alone. 'When the pupil is ready, the master appears.' But the master is not to be obsessively sought.

Yet the final relationship is love.

As one progresses in spirituality, some gifts of the psychic may well be bestowed, and they have their value as beacons of encouragement. They have been notably bestowed within the Charismatic Movement which has had its value in reviving an otherwise staid conventional Church. The danger here is that those so endowed begin to present themselves with an aura of religious superiority, as if they were better than their fellows. Gifts of the spirit can all too easily inflate the personality without integrating it. Sadly this has split congregations, whilst undoubtedly benefiting many. The essential ingredient as always is love. When this is absent or inadequate, things fall apart. The true gifts of the spirit are as described by St Paul, love, joy, peace, longsuffering, gentleness, goodness, faithfulness, meekness and temperance.

How do we differentiate between the authority from above and the 'hunch' or prejudice that is within us? We need to remember our own unimportance. A test is how put out we may be by others who challenge us. Another test is our sense of humour. The more we can accept ourselves with levity the sounder our motives are likely to be. How does one progress spiritually? 'By love may He be gotten and holden; by thought never.'

In the closing paragraphs Martin Israel describes the final steps in the path to his ordination as a deacon – a precarious path in his case. He did not know his future path, as none of us knows ours. But if we follow the truth, he assures us, it will lead 'from the unreal to the real, from darkness to light, from death to immortality.'

6. Smouldering Fire – The Work of the Holy Spirit

This book, the third in the series of Martin Israel's main published works, deals with the problem of good and evil, and their reconciliation with Christ through the Spirit. Rather than focus upon the Charismatic Renewal, popular at that time, the author felt that something else was required. He deals not only with the psychological and the psychical aspects of spiritual life, but also the whole journey from the birth of spiritual awareness through the facing of evil, personal death, and the rebirth of a new person.

To be born is to become aware of one's own independent existence. God created us as independent beings out of the void so that He might love us and receive our love in return. It began with our creation and ends when we return of our own freewill to the Creator. He gives His only Son that everyone who has faith may not die, but have eternal life. The inanimate creature is scarcely aware of its separation from the Creator. It is only when mankind is formed that this separation becomes meaningful. As part of our growth we become aware of this. We must learn the principles of diversity that govern creation. This takes time. The process is embodied in the Book of Genesis, though it would be absurd to try and relate the Biblical account of creation to our modern scientific understanding of the world and of evolution. We are now more fully aware of the universe in which we exist, though there is a mystic element in Holy Scripture that still has meaning. At the end of Genesis Chapter 4 it is recorded, 'At that time mankind began to invoke the Lord by name.' Religion had begun, and would reach its ultimate destiny in the New Jerusalem, where there is no Temple because the Word of God dwells there.

Birth – Natural and Spiritual

The Spirit of God infuses all living creatures including mankind, and we become capable of progressing by experience in a world of time and space. Unfortunately many people function at so low a level of consciousness that their ego does not develop beyond an awareness of bodily needs and comforts. But when they take the step of responding to a call to faith, however limited in scope, they begin to adopt their true identity.

To be centred upon oneself is necessary for survival, and is an essential part of childhood. But if that child receives its due measure of love and acceptance then it will begin to realise that its true identity extends beyond the mere physical body, and will begin to progress toward adulthood. Yet we have to mature still further, such that we can withstand the blows of misfortune. It is through the Spirit of God, of which we may seldom be aware, that we can grow and that the spirit within us can become informed. This is especially so when we have to make moral choices. It is the Holy Spirit that summons us from simple and often dull conformity to a life of challenge through to hidden promise. The ultimate victory may not be a temporal one, but a victory of the spirit over the flesh which is the stuff of eternal life.

The Spirit of God and the spirit within ourselves are not identical, yet neither are they totally separate. The spirit within us is what drives us. Medical science can orient the body towards healing but it cannot heal. This is undertaken by the Spirit of God pulsating within us, as wondrous a miracle as any in Holy Scripture. These miracles of healing can occur 'in the twinkling of an eye'. Yet there is a destructive psyche within us that may frustrate the power of the Spirit.

But what of those who have been denied love and acceptance? Whilst psychotherapy may help them, yet paradoxically they may on their own rise above their meagre inheritance, and even because of it. When deprived of all outer support, they may then come to know and to accept themselves, in the absence of anything else. It can be a delight to meet and know such people, few though they be, and they number among them the leaders of mankind. A life that is able to look forward to all experiences, good and bad, as part of growth into a full person will achieve true identity. Birth thus has three components. There is the physical birth, when we leave our mother's womb. There may be personal birth when we make an essential moral choice that determines our future. Finally there is spiritual birth, when the Word of God informs us of our full identity, that of a Child of God. This Word lies dormant in us, like a seed, until the moment of its germination. Then we truly know who we are.

The Birth into Spiritual Awareness

The Prophet Ezekiel records his vision in which the dry bones, representing the body of the people of Israel, are transformed into life although crushed under the yoke of the Babylonian captivity. This is the way of spiritual rebirth for the individual. Paradoxically birth follows death. We have to 'die' before we can know God. The Spirit only descends upon those who have given their all or who are so crushed by adversity that they are truly open to receive it. Thus life is a dangerous adventure. Yet the Spirit of God knocks at our door and enters if invited with trust and thanksgiving. Some live a life of selfish luxury until some event, such as a Near-Death Experience, affords them a chance totally to review their true purpose and to make amends. Jesus tells the Parable of the Prodigal Son to illustrate how meaning can suddenly come into a life that has lost its purpose. Yet the most revealing part of this tale is the wilful movement of the importunate son from his life of conformity toward his destiny, albeit upon a downward slope. This is his authentic birth as an individual, from which his ultimate growth as a full person stems. When we finally 'come to ourselves', this is when the Spirit of God enters our personality.

This does not mean that a Spirit-filled life necessarily proceeds along well-defined tracks bringing success and prosperity. On the contrary it may lead into a maze of unexplored passages, each one having something to teach us. But even when we feel we are utterly lost we are impelled by a sense of purpose that shows itself in hope and expectation. The action of the Holy Spirit cannot be invoked by the will. Techniques do not help us. The Spirit itself decides how and when it will bestow itself.

The Holy Spirit is sometimes described as the feminine principle of the Trinity, though this of course is symbolic, for all the Persons combine both the male and the female. The Spirit is courteous and does not take us over, since free choice is the divine gift to us. But when we accept the Spirit, we also take on responsibilities and the growth into perfection begins in earnest.

The Consecration of the Will

Many are called but few are chosen. To find the road to authentic life is hard, and in each generation only a few appear to be selected as natural mystics. For these people nothing suffices but the vision of God. This might seem unfair but for the fact that this vision can only be obtained by experiencing the depths of life as well as the heights. Moreover the spiritually unaware are not necessarily destined to remain in that state forever. As we become aware of such meagre talents as we have, sanctification becomes within our grasp. Indeed great gifts can themselves become a snare if we allow ourselves to become inflated with self-satisfaction and so lose contact with the Spirit.

If we are called, then we become eligible to bear the suffering of the world. This is not comforting but it can be invigorating for it gives us purpose. The reverse side of this vocation is commitment, which enables the Holy Spirit to enter us and direct our lives. This commitment may oblige us to renounce our previous life totally and to begin anew, but more often we are called to pursue the existing 'daily round' but with a new vision and purpose.

Faith is a gift of the Spirit. Through it we may aspire to heights of endeavour. But we ourselves have to put it into practice; it is not done for us. If we do this, the Spirit will support us with an inner assurance that goodness lies at the heart of reality. Sometimes the Holy Spirit comes to us when we seem to be in comfort and safety, to wake us to a course of action that may initially be far from sound or provident. It may only be after we have faced the corruption that lies within us that we can receive the refining love of God. Then the Holy Spirit can begin to work within us.

Descent into Darkness

It is said that Jesus was led into the wilderness to be tempted by the devil. The devil in this instance can be interpreted in a number of ways. There is the devil within us, which lies quiet until our security is threatened and it then unleashes itself. But there is also the devil of divisiveness that thrives in a competitive world. An unappeased person can display such a degree of hatred that total destruction can result if his or her actions are not curbed. Spasms of genocide in our own modern world are all too obvious instances of this. We have to face reality in our own wilderness for it is there that we are completely alone. The power of silence is a purifying one, although it can be terrifying, for we then come to terms with our true nature. It can be a mistake to equate the presence of the Holy Spirit with peace, prosperity and happiness that may go with a conventional life and religious observance. Christ brings not peace but a sword, and we have to be prepared for this. Having confronted the true shadow side of our personality we have to wait in patience and in the silence of prayer for healing to begin. There is no short cut to the spiritual life. But having led us to the depths we are given the power to work with God towards the redemption of that which is evil. The true disciple is always in the wilderness because that is where so much of the work has to be done.

The spiritual path leads us through darkness, which we have to face and recognise in ourselves. It is only then that the Holy Spirit can become active in our lives, bringing healing.

The Regeneration of the Personality

The work of the Holy Spirit in regenerating our diseased personality is one of the most important aspects of the spiritual life. Our will cannot do it alone, yet nor can the Spirit operate without the wholehearted support of our will. This was probably why Jesus could work few miracles in Nazareth where he was known too well for people to be open to His mystical powers. We need to have a simple openness to the magnanimity of God.

The human personality has a vast range, from the animal – necessary for our survival – to the spiritual within us. We become aware of our unworthiness, but this will not help us on an intellectual level alone. Indeed it may lead to despair. Jesus came down to our level and even seemed to enjoy the company of those who sinned openly, loving them for what they were. 'I come not to call the righteous, but sinners, to repentance.' He came not to judge, and still less to condemn. For our souls to be healed we must first accept what we are. Inability to do this lies at the heart of the most deadly of sins -

the sin of pride. Sometimes this pride has its roots in some earlier betrayal, the memory of which has first to be healed before progress can be made.

God loves us as we stand. Sometimes we wrestle with some weakness that we feel separates us from God. Yet God loves us because of our weaknesses. We may reject God, though not primarily through the mind, for often our view of God is distorted. We have to accept and even love our weaknesses, bearing them as if they were our personal crosses that we have to bear. We may pray for their removal, yet we have to contend inwardly with them as they stand. In wrestling with our dark forces we may seek the support of professionals such as psychotherapists who are well acquainted with sin and what it can do. For whatever is done to relieve pain or dispel ignorance is inspired by the Spirit of God. But only when we have the courage, honesty, humility and faith to face our shortcomings can we progress so that our personality regenerates.

The Spirit as Healer

Healing is the binding together of the disintegrated person into a transformed whole. The Holy Spirit is the power that integrates, and it acts from within, slowly and progressively. Cure of a physical or mental disability, which may occur quickly, is not to be equated with the healing of the personality. Jesus' healing ministry demonstrated the experience of God's love as a beginning. Two of the essentials were forgiveness and faith. This faith is not a blind compulsive belief. It is more a relaxing of the personality in warmth, admitting my own ignorance but accepting my place in the scheme of things. The forgiveness of sins is a natural result of a faith that will not shrink from exposure to God 'to whom all hearts are open'. As we are forgiven, so we are open to the love of God, and are not motivated by fear or a sense of duty, but an overruling concern for others. Good works that come from our personal selves are inevitably tainted with a need for personal recognition or some other factor which will limit their effectiveness.

The Spirit works best in human relationships, as when Jesus was baptised by John the Baptist. The healing Spirit does not remain still. He impels us onward to the fulfilment of our destiny. Anyone who has been truly healed by the Spirit is obliged to lead a new life. This is the price we pay, and if we fail to pay it, healing may be withdrawn. Unless we have learned something about ourselves as the result of our suffering our healing will not be full. Jesus asked the cripple, 'Do you want to be healed?' Acceptance of the price is not to be taken for granted.

Many people who practise what is sometimes rather dubiously called 'spiritual healing' tend to concentrate upon one particular malady or circumstance rather than the healing of the whole person. If they did attempt the whole healing, they would have to face also the disorder within themselves, which not everyone is prepared to do. 'Physician heal thyself' is the challenge that faces all who seek to heal others. The Spirit works through others, but works best through those who are emptiest of self-opinion and of the kind of 'holy arrogance' that accompanies some kinds of dogmatic religion.

The Spirit and the Psyche

Do not trust every spirit, says St John, for there are many prophets falsely inspired. If the psyche can be equated with the mind of an individual, the psychic field of mankind is the collective experience of the whole human race. Carl Jung speaks of a 'collective unconscious' that unites our ancestors' primitive thoughts and fears with our own instinctive reactions, and it is clear that 'no man is an island'. We are in fellowship with the hopes and fears of our fellows, and it is in this sense that Jesus took upon himself the psychic burden of the whole world, past present and future, when He was crucified.

St Paul urges us to be humble, gentle, patient, forbearing and charitable. Mankind was created to be a god reflecting the nature of our Creator and we shall not find peace until we find the Christhood within us.

Many people have a degree of psychic awareness and can communicate in a non-rational way with the world about us. This is good provided it is selfless, but it can all too easily be used to project our ego in harmful ways. The psychic world is a vast conglomeration of mental attitudes and emotional forces that are manipulated by those who inhabit that world. It is intrinsically no more evil than our own physical world but because of its nebulous nature, it cannot easily be grasped. It is alternately a world of sublime aspiration and of dangerous delusion. Yet it is the simple soul that can sometimes attain psychic awareness. The little child can on occasion perceive the unreliability of an adult that experienced adults will miss.

The psychic field is thus to be understood as the realm of insubstantial forms that emanate from the living and the dead, and may be numbered with 'the Communion of Saints' although the true Communion has committed itself to the service of God. If we avoid the intermediate spirits which can lead us astray, the Spirit of God can communicate with us through the Communion of Saints. But first our minds must be still, and secondly we must be free of disturbing intermediate spirits.

The Psychic Gifts of the Holy Spirit

The gifts of the Spirit as enumerated in I Corinthians 12 are wise speech, putting the deepest knowledge into words, faith, gifts of healing, miraculous powers, prophecy, distinguishing true spirits from false, ecstatic utterances of various kinds, and the ability to interpret. They are distributed separately to each individual at the will of the Spirit, the basis of which is a freeing from the rational mind so that the psychic faculty can be opened up. As we become liberated from childhood prejudices we begin to know ourselves better and can better relate to others.

Some people accept the gifts of the Spirit as a direct communication from God. This may be something of a simplification, for in the hands of immature people these gifts can lead to bigotry. It is a spiritual law that those who are in communion with God become more Christ-like in their everyday lives so that 'by their fruits ye shall know them.'

Psychic powers are a natural endowment. We all have them to some degree but those specially gifted, called 'sensitives', possess these gifts to a marked degree. Children are often gifted more so than adults, possibly because they are less analytical. Yet it is necessary that adulthood shall develop and so that these gifts shall decline. This may be disappointing, yet it is part of the maturing of the soul that the ego shall develop in order that we shall later share it with the whole community. We are to attain union with God as free agents and not by a kind of fusion in which our selves are merged. We have first to know ourselves before we can offer ourselves, and the aim of the spiritual life is not to destroy the ego but to fulfil it by allowing it to mature. The spiritually aspiring person should be at ease with themselves and joyfully accepting what they are, whilst recognising their weaknesses in a positive manner. When the Holy Spirit is working with us, our ego becomes strengthened but we become more aware of others so that we can reach out to them. The gift of tongues (termed glossolalia) is valuable in that, if we have this gift, it may enable us to communicate simply with God in a manner similar to an infant making its first contact with its parents, and we are told we must receive the kingdom of heaven as a little child. If used properly it gives us greater peace and silence. It is only when such gifts are in the hands of immature people that harm can result in that exhibitionism can take over, and a desire to impress others, or even a form of escapism. On balance it is better used in private than in public gatherings, save among groups who know each other well and have passed beyond the demands of personal recognition.

Another gift much sought after is that of healing, which can be very beneficial. There are many natural healers, and this is clearly a psychic gift. Some have the ability to make us feel better just by being there, bringing hope with which to dispel anxiety. They may be quite unaware of their gift. Another class of healer claims contact with specific psychic entities such as 'spirit guides' and these should not be rejected out of hand. The angelic hierarchy, although often a subject of latter-day Christian unbelief, is clearly involved in this realm. Those who cannot but reject all talk of the psychic realm as nonsense would be advised not to reject it totally. It might be wise to set it aside in the recesses of one's mind and allow it to remain, possibly for many years. It may be that in due course some unexpected event will cause us to re-evaluate what we have learnt in the light of new experience.

The healing gifts of the Spirit have a natural, a psychical and a divine component and they all come from God the Holy Spirit. Whereas a natural healer may tend to take the credit and fall into pride, and the psychic healer become dominated by the spirit guides who are involved, the healer who is directed by God works free of self-centredness and is one with eternity. He or she can function as a balanced person.

The Spirit in the World

The Holy Spirit comes fully into our lives when we are ready to receive Him. He does not overwhelm us. Moreover He is working not alone but with the Communion of Saints that comprises not only those who have passed on but those who aspire to know God on earth. I begin to know myself when I have shed all selfish concerns. And if I offer myself, even to death, I shall gain knowledge of the eternal that is within me. This is a key teaching of the mystics in all religions.

Jesus came into the world as a light for the spiritually blind. Mankind needed to be brought back from the meaninglessness of the ages. To effect this, the Word of God spoke through many teachers, notably the saints of India and the Buddha, not to mention the philosophers of Ancient Greece. Each had an individual light to shine, related to the needs of the day. The Buddha had no use for a personal God, realising the harm that personal representations of God can do. But this leads to a cold religion that can ignore the issues of everyday. The religion of Israel was prophetic in inspiration and spoke to the people through its prophets and teachers, acknowledging the love and the hatred in life though they could look forward to little other than Sheol, a wraith-like existence, since pre-exilic Judaism had little to say about life after death. Exposure to other faiths such as Persian, Babylonian and Greek thought prepared them for a wider appreciation of life beyond death, whereas the Hindu/Buddhist traditions had taken immortality as a major feature of reality. The life of Jesus brought the way, the truth and the life to mankind in such a degree that 'no man comes to the Father save through the Son.' It is a sad fact that once

Christianity attained temporal power it declined from its heritage of love and charity to become an instrument of persecution. And so the Word of God then spoke through the Arabian prophet Mohammed. Whilst non-Muslims cannot easily relate to the violence and absolutism within this faith, yet it certainly brought about a civilisation and culture through the dark ages of barbarism and Christian bigotry. By the end of the Middle Ages the Spirit of God was working through many men, who by that time were liberated from the constraints of authoritarian religion such that they could aspire to a scientific understanding of their surroundings.

The Word of God has never lacked a mouthpiece. Today it is recognised that He speaks through the scientist, the philosopher and the artist as well as the theologian. There is no sentimentality about the Spirit. As one mode of communication has become outdated for its purpose it is replaced by another. As limitations of thought have become apparent other vehicles have been used, not all of which can be equated with the higher religions. When atheistic materialism was at its height in the nineteenth century, the Spiritualistic movement was created. And whilst much of this movement has foundered on the rocks of triviality, it has given rise to a number of responsible organisations that conduct serious research into psychic matters and the evidence for an after-life. Another movement that started at that time was Christian Science, when the Churches' mission to heal was at its lowest. It brought calmness and positive thought to a world of stress and anxiety. But even this is not the whole truth. Another mode of thought is modern Theosophy, with its emphasis on meditation, linking Eastern and Western religious thought.

Arguably four contemporary modes of thought each have their contribution to make: Atheistic Humanism, Spiritualism, Christian Science and Theosophy. Atheism develops mankind's self-reliance. Spiritualism broadens our grasp of reality. Christian Science exalts the value of faith. Theosophy stresses the intellectual grasp of things. Without the Spirit of God each of these is inadequate. With the Spirit of God, however, each can progress beyond any restraining doctrines they may have and can inspire believer and unbeliever alike.

The Serving Spirit

The Holy Spirit is truly alive in someone when they are no longer centred upon their own life and personal benefit. We do not need to seek to assert ourselves nor to justify ourselves to the world at large. We know an inner peace. Our internal balance has been established so that we can adopt an attitude of equanimity, sometimes termed 'holy indifference'. We can meet with triumph or disaster without totally forfeiting inner calm and serenity. The Spirit brings us love, joy, peace, patience, kindness, goodness, faithfulness, gentleness and self-control.

We can be ourselves without needing to possess things or people to justify ourselves. The advocates of many modern spiritual movements unfortunately live for results, and this means they are seriously incomplete. The same may be said of some who have an excess of missionary zeal within the higher religions. They attract those who are unsure of themselves, claiming to have a monopoly of truth and threatening damnation to those who fail to accept their way of thought. When they do this, the one Person they exclude is the Holy Spirit Itself. The saint on the other hand sacrifices material comfort, security, reputation if necessary to follow the truth into the wilderness, returning to share that truth with those who will receive it. Is all dogma therefore wrong? Not really, because it affords a structure within which saint and mystic can thrive. True dogma is the way of abundant life. So what is true dogma? Is it Buddhist, Hindu, Islamic, Jewish or Christian? The answer is that it is all these great religious systems if properly understood and lived, for their saints and mystics have shown that each way leads to communion with God. But one needs to remember that 'the written law condemns to death, but the Spirit gives life.'

Are all the higher religions of equal value? In the power of the Spirit and within the logic of mysticism any number of propositions has their own validity in the truth whose nature is that of God. Each of the higher religions has their own priceless gifts to bestow. The German Universalist philosopher G. E. Lessing tells the tale of a father who bequeathed a precious ring to his favourite son. This ring had the power to bless the life of whoever wore it. But the father had two other sons whom he could not bear to deprive, so he fashioned two identical rings for each of them. When he died there was strife among the sons as to who had the true ring, so they consulted a wise man, who himself also could not distinguish the one ring from the others. He advised that only by the quality of the life they led would the sons know who had the true ring, so each should strive to lead the good life to the best of his ability. Lessing applied this parable to Judaism, Christianity and Islam, though it could be applied to many other faiths as well.

The Spirit of Prayer

The Spirit of God speaks through whomsoever He chooses without enquiring into beliefs or pedigree. The Word of God is a seed implanted into us at birth from which the Spirit can lead if allowed to do so, bringing us into contact with the Christ. Yet without the Creator Father and the Word of God, the Spirit would have nowhere to lead us to, so this is why the Trinity is of such significance. But we need to open ourselves by worship and by service to mankind. This is the practice of prayer. Prayer is the act of self-giving and renunciation. It is the very opposite of grasping for spiritual things and gifts. A person gives themselves to God in humble adoration.

True religion aims at spiritualising matter but not imprisoning God within it. Dame Julian of Norwich says that God is the ground of our beseeching, or in modern language the foundation of our prayer. The meeting-place of prayer is the silence that comes when we realise how inadequate we are. Bereft of pride, we can then speak to God. The result of our speaking is the outpouring of the Holy Spirit. Prayer is the inner response of the soul to God. It may be solitary or else shared communally. Arguably effective prayer depends upon three aspects: something that has been brought in when we were conceived, a discipline of meditation, and work in the world.

The discipline of prayer is learned primarily from example from others, so religious tradition is important. Meditation without direction can lead to a separation into a personal world of self-delusion. Meditation can be achieved in groups, but the best of meditation is done in a full religious body where everyone worships God. Liturgy and sacrament is very important too. A service may be inspiring but in the end worship or liturgy is its own reward. Sacraments remind us of the holiness of matter.

The end of prayer is union with God. The more complete the religion the more balanced and perfect is the prayer. And the end of religion is the divination of mankind so we make real the divine image that is within us. In the mystical life we come to realise that every creature is in psychic contact with every other creature. When a group or an individual intercedes with love for a fellow person in trouble the Spirit of Christ is among the intercessors and communes with the one who is in difficulty. The Spirit can guide if we have the humility and patience to wait in silence. Asking means enquiring about the nature of our difficulty. Seeking is giving up everything for the kingdom of God. Knocking means giving up or changing our attitude to life. Then the Spirit will come and open us to reality.

Humility and the Spirit

Humility is not a matter of stressing to everybody how humble or inadequate we are. Paradoxically that can be a way of exalting ourselves. Humility is more a matter of self-forgetfulness, where we become too concerned with the matter in hand to be aware of our humility or the lack of it.

The fruits of pride – the opposite of humility – are insensitivity to others, arrogance, self-righteousness and an inability to receive love. Pride holds us in fixed attitudes. We cannot tolerate the prospect of our being mistaken. Sadly, pride often afflicts the very religious and those who aspire to spiritual knowledge. The Spirit of God cannot enter the soul of a proud person. The proud are often quite unaware of their arrogance, and if religious they will persist intrusively in seeking to save the souls of others. Indeed if anyone challenges this kind of person they will be dismissed as fools or scoundrels. In politics it is the proud who aspire to the various forms of dictatorship. Regrettably the same attitude has been true within the world's major religions.

The aim of the spiritual life is to prepare in each moment for the full development of the real person, both today and in the life hereafter. God will not allow us to perish. There is life after death, but what survives depends in no small measure to what we do with our lives on earth. The various great religions have their own perceptions of survival. I myself look for the survival of all creatures through the knowledge of the love of God, but this is not an easy option. The full process of redemption will call for much purification and learning in the life to come.

So what is our duty to our unawakened brethren? Do we evangelise or ignore? Arguably neither is right on its own. If we want to share the good news with those outside our circle we must follow the call of the Holy Spirit to communicate joyfully with troubled souls, to bind up the broken hearted. And before we try and remove the speck in another's eye we must first remove the beam in our own, after which we may see clearly how to proceed. Carl Jung teaches never to try and convert a patient, but to bring them to the point where they can see ahead for themselves. Salvation is the bringing of a soul into the state of health. Over-zealous revivalism, however well meant, can work on the emotions of the unbalanced, and this can be unsound.

The true Christ shows us the way. He humbles Himself to take on the ignominy of the meanest criminal. No one comes to God save through this way and the call is always the same, 'follow me'.

The Fulfilling Spirit

We function on three levels: the physical, the psychical and the spiritual. All are equally important, even though the spiritual may take priority, since this involves communion with God. The Holy Spirit brings about a renewal of the whole person, and this leads to a greater psychic sensitivity. But without a corresponding increase of the intellect this can lead to demonic possession unless these sensitivities are dedicated to God's service. Some religious groups become obsessed with a fight against what they feel are the demonic forces in the world, yet do not realise that they themselves are projecting some of these forces. By contrast the genuinely inspired person, although aware of demonic forces, is not overwhelmed by them. The Spirit-filled person has a consciousness far above the lower reaches of the unconscious.

When we know God in our hearts as well as with reason we understand that love is the supreme property of life, and this calls for our assent. But in receiving the Holy Spirit it is 'Thy will, not mine, be done.' A mystical experience cannot be cultivated. Those who attempt spiritual enlightenment intent only on self-development will not reach the Promised Land until they have first come to know themselves. But then the fruit of spiritual identity is joy, which leads to true communion with God and with the whole of creation – the meaning of heaven.

In the spiritual life there is a phase in which we must pass beyond physical relationships, rewarding though they be, to a kind of chastity that allows further growth within the wider relationships that heaven opens up.

Transfiguration

The transfiguration of the body into the quality of eternal spirit is the end to which growth proceeds. When our bodies have been so transfigured the Holy Spirit enables us to participate in the whole created universe. The transfigured Christ is in communion with the risen spirits of Moses and Elijah, who symbolise the law and the prophets. The three disciples who were privileged to see Christ transfigured on earth were told for the time being not to tell anyone what they had seen.

Transfiguration brings about a change in the person, who may be entrusted to carry out some special task. Yet the full effect may only gradually become apparent in their outer life. There may be an increased transparency in the body of one who has been transfigured. Saints have traditionally been depicted as having an aura or halo, and those gifted with clairvoyant skills can often perceive the aura of other people. They can often also discern the physical, mental and spiritual state by the manner in which the aura appears. The transfigured person has a spiritual light, but of a kind different from certain kinds of self-centred 'charming' people who can be deceiving in their demeanour. They too have a kind of light, but one that needs to be recognised for what it is. For the essential quality of transfiguration is openness, and receptivity to the Holy Spirit. The true prophet becomes a cleansed person, who can speak the direct word of God, and who is in mystical union with God. And it is the mystic's task to bring to earth what has been shown to him or her, which is often not a message of comfort.

In the realm of transfiguration there is much to be said about healing, which though it may be physical is primarily about transformation of the whole personality. Healing may be gradual, for pent up emotions have first to be released. And the constitution of the would-be saint must first be ready. St Augustine was not merely being immature when he prayed to be given chastity but not yet. Though when the disciple has learned to accept the common task in the face of all difficulty, then the ascetic life is no burden and becomes one of unbounded joy.

Confrontation

The end of the spiritual life is failure in the worldly sense, but a new spiritual creation. It is a death that leads to a fuller life, as when the child 'dies' to its parents' enclosed world in order to progress to the wider challenge of schooling. Again it happens when the young person leaves home. And again still it may happen when we have to pass through the trauma of bereavement. The secret is that death means the end of a limited view of life, through which we become able to open up new ways and gifts. Not that this is pleasant. We cannot escape the dark side of life that has to be endured. The light of the Spirit is never extinguished but neither has it overcome the darkness of this world.

The remarkable intelligence of mankind has in our generation brought about a striking increase in our life expectancy, be it a blessing or a curse according to the nature of our life story. Dame Julian of Norwich reminds us of her revelation, 'It is behoved that there should be sin, but all shall be well, and all shall be well, and all manner of thing shall be well.'

The Triumph of Evil

To those who are spiritually aware, death comes as a gateway to a fuller life. To some it comes slowly, to others suddenly. And to some, misfortune occurs in this life. Why should that be? Firstly no one is exempt from bearing their share of the sins of the world. Secondly, misfortune, if borne with courage, can strengthen the character. And the saintly person has first to know degradation before they can know God, and this can involve loss of contact with the faith that one had. ('My God, why hast thou forsaken me?') The attitude of Jesus on the Cross was more than mere acceptance and forgiveness. It was identification with the evils of the world. To those who are spiritually aspiring, preparation is necessary before one can adopt the ultimate in austerity. The new gift of the Spirit at the Crucifixion was the ability to take on every vice and perversion that had existed since the foundation of the world, and though vanquished, to triumph so that good men and women rejoiced.

Peace

Before peace can come to mankind each of us must know exactly who we are and what we stand for. This was what Jesus perceived with all who came in contact with him, differentiating between the traditionally good who were self-righteous and the 'sinful' tax gatherer who had faced himself and aspired to something more. In bringing not peace but a sword, Jesus exposed the polarities of good and evil in a way which was totally new, and He inevitably perished by the sword.

Yet above the struggle between good and evil is the truth of the spiritual radiance that emanates from the risen Christ. He is 'the peace of God that passeth all man's understanding.' A new Christ has appeared, at peace and glowing with joy, beyond the polarities of good and evil. He blesses the world in a love that knows no bounds, and looks toward the New Jerusalem, which needs no sun nor moon, nor a temple because God Himself will dwell there and provide all that it requires. The great mystics knew well that God is beyond good and evil. The great souls of the past have shown us the way but they cannot do our work for us. We have the duty and joy to continue what they have started and bring it to completion. Then in the words of Isaiah, peace shall come and 'They shall not hurt or destroy in all my holy mountain, for as the waters cover the sea, so shall the land be filled with the knowledge of the Lord.'

7. The Pain that Heals

Martin Israel here deals with the place that suffering has in the growth of the person, and at the end of each chapter there is a paragraph to aid meditation.

The problem of evil in the face of a loving God is not something that can be solved purely at an intellectual level. In this strange life, he says, we grow through adversity rather than by success. Worldly wisdom teaches us to win. The spiritual path teaches us how to be good and gracious losers. Suffering can be creative and there is a wider ministry of healing than that which merely exists to smooth out life's difficulties.

The Many Faces of Pain

Misfortune strikes unexpectedly, in the form of sudden illness, disappointment, agonising news or something else of that kind. We realise how little control we have over our affairs. Much of the time we are merely concerned with our physical body and daily affairs. Pain can then be a great awakener. Human life, though it may have much surface glitter, is in part essentially dark and this has to be faced. The first experience of suffering that most of us experience is physical pain. Part of this may be positive in that it draws our attention to a part of our body that is amiss and needs treatment. But this is an oversimplification. Severity of pain does not always equate with degree of illness, and heavy continuing pain can be debilitating. There is little spiritual growth in this. But the message of physical pain can be communicated to others.

Then there is mental agony. This can be far more terrible, partly because it cannot easily be communicated or shared. Our lives may have been devoted to something that can no longer be seen as a reality. A particular part of this is the moral component. Guilt can be especially debilitating, until we have managed to face up to failings and to acknowledge them. Another factor is fear, and especially the fear of rejection, and the fear of the loss of a loved one. So long as we are limited to ourselves we shall be imprisoned in pain of one sort or another.

Journey into Truth

Suffering can concentrate the mind, and to begin with we are preoccupied with ourselves. First we may be surrounded with support, but then our friends recede. Suffering is to be seen as disharmony between ourselves and the spirit of God. We then come to realise that suffering can be seen as the way in which our will is chastened so that it may eventually embark upon that which is good. We are of course driven by many self-centred powers within us. To break this stranglehold most of us need the rigour of a religious discipline. Without this, we tend to end up in idle fantasy of one kind or another. But once our enlightened will is awakened and consecrated we are free to become truly ourselves. The person who returns after great suffering is changed and can themselves change the world round about. Once we have lost our personal possessions we can begin to know those things that are eternal. This does not mean that we should eschew the possessions that God has given us, but merely that we should not cling to them.

Then, what of those who have not experienced a measure of pain? Should they feel guilty? No, but they should give thanks for what they have and be vigilant in looking out for others who have suffered. Most people will have their allotted quota of pain in due course. Such is the human condition. But if we remember God throughout our lives then our suffering will merge into happiness and joy, which is the preserve of the world's saints.

When tragedy strikes there may be indignation and revolt, followed by darkness, and the need for solid toil in the cold light of reality, until the eternal centre of truth becomes revealed. This truth lies within each of us until it becomes apparent. Then we can start to move towards a complete re-creation of our personality. St Paul tells us that the sufferings we now endure are nothing compared to the splendour that awaits us.

The Dark Face of Reality

There are two types of people. There are those who accept a spiritual world. And there are those whose acceptance is restricted to a material world and to whom the idea of a God is incomprehensible. The first group are not necessarily any better than the second. Yet at least they can be assured of a wider and thus more authentic existence than those whose sphere is restricted to the limits of the human mind, and what can be demonstrated by science or by reason. The spiritually aware person is open to the Spirit of God and to eternal truth rather than being bound by material fact.

Material folk can have their eyes opened. Usually this happens when they have a spiritual experience, and this may arise through suffering. Spiritual people may also have their eyes opened wider in this way, and may indeed resist, for this usually involves suffering also, or by the experience of darkness that most of us would prefer not to undergo. This darkness may involve letting go of all our previously held ideas or prejudices. The movement forward from this point is voluntary, and may seem to follow a pre-ordained path, but nonetheless it is a wilderness. Jesus Christ himself faced a trial of this kind before His ministry could commence. We each have an ego, or a part of us that is basically self-centred. Our ego is a loyal servant when we are a full person, but our ego can be a demon if we allow it to be master of us.

There is also the reality of God, which has a dark as well as a light side, although it is probably more helpful to consider the darkness as the 'reverse side' of a God of light and love. Jacob in the Bible had to struggle with the angel of God. 'I have seen God face to face and my life has been spared'. In the real tests of life we come to know God. For the law of life is toil and travail. To grow we must bear it with courage and faith.

A Devouring Fire

The fire of God, like earthly fire, both devours and purifies. That which is transitory is consumed. Whatever is of permanent value is cleansed and renewed. I believe however that much of what appears to be ephemeral and so much dross is ultimately refined and redeemed in the end. Those of us who seek to achieve our true identity face a lot of work. We are surrounded from birth by circumstances that tend to tie us to worldly affairs. This is especially so in affluent societies. We grow up in families and graduate to other friendships and collegiate groups. But much of this is selfish. Eventually we face ageing, disease and death. Have we the reserves built up with which to face these events? Few people can easily face solitude.

To know ourselves takes an acceptance of ourselves as we really are. Once we have reached this self-knowledge it is warm and comforting, but to get there one faces the surrounding darkness. Techniques such as meditation can induce a feeling of warmth and comfort, but not all of this is sound. Our inner feelings are often a poor guide to our spiritual progress. The true path is one of renunciation. We have to leave all behind, and most of us have no enthusiasm for taking this path until our souls, energised by the Holy Spirit, thrust us in that direction. The journey to God is also the journey into hell. In our case this is the journey into the facing of the darkness in our own personality. Many sectarian religionists are obsessed with perceptions of the devil, which they project upon others with whom they disagree. In reality the devil is the darkness that lies within each of us, which has to be confronted and overcome. Then the spark of the divine which lies also within us is enabled to burst into a flame of illumination.

The Hell Within

Hell has traditionally been regarded as a place, where wicked souls go. But this is far too simplistic. The soul does not need to go anywhere. Hell is a psychic state of mind. It works towards our isolation and death. And yet it is a necessary part of us. As in the Tao philosophy, we have the positive direction or Yang as well as the negative force of Yin. When the two are in balance then progress and creativity can continue. Suffering comprises two kinds of pain: the outer pain of loss and the inner pain of self-discovery. It is the inner pain that leads us into our own internal hell. Then we realise how lonely we are. It is possible to be alone in the midst of friends and family. Our private hell contains a throng of demons: anger, hatred, jealousy, and a general death-wish. Whenever we are thwarted they come to the surface. They behave like spoilt children and cause us to behave abominably to our fellows. If we hold positions of authority we then procure that there is corporate hell of one kind or another.

We need to come to an inner core of reconciled reality. Until we do so we shall always seek earthly possessions. Suffering may be necessary to rid us of these encumbrances so that we can embrace the true word of God and the total destruction of the selfish side of our ego, which may well be achieved in our progress after death.

An Encounter with Fear

Fear can paralyse us and lead us to choose the status quo, as being usually the safest option. In adopting prudence, fear is the negative pole. We look before we leap, and this is sound. But inordinate fear can paralyse and is basically demonic in character. However much we have, we fear to lose it, and bury it in the ground like the man in the parable with one talent. We all have to take risks, and if we do so, using our inner gifts of discernment and intuition, it can lead on to our growth into maturity.

In one sense fear is an essential prerequisite of love. Until we know fear, we do not open ourselves to the love and providence of God. The tiny child cries immediately upon leaving the womb and entering the world, before opening itself to the wonders of the world. It then has to learn that the love shown it by parents is not necessarily present in the outer spheres of life. It may even meet disturbed people who emanate a diabolical psychic atmosphere that is negative and terrifying in itself. Fortunately this is not the whole picture and there are many beneficent influences in society. Yet it is true that the more a child is surrounded by positive souls the easier it is for that child to grow positively itself.

There is however a much more sinister fear that can virtually annihilate a person. That is the kind of fear that emanates from prison camps and follows cruel treatment by unjust wicked people. Punishment, if it is remorseless, tortures the body and humiliates the personality, sometimes burying itself in the unconscious mind so that the victim fears and cannot remember the source of the fear. The person so humiliated is often not compatible with others and is generally inconvenient for others to deal with, so that those unaffected will shun the victim. As with the Parable of the Samaritan, we tend to pass by on the other side. And so we ourselves fear this rejection, which is a terrible fear to bear. It is related to the fear of bereavement, or the end of a deep relationship.

The ultimate fear is to be enveloped in such darkness that we cease to be separate beings, and our ego is on the point of extinction. It is the terror of Christ in Gethsemane. Yet paradoxically those who have experienced it are highly privileged. They can understand the meaning of resurrection, and a great truth has been revealed to them about the ultimate nature of reality. This is the path of life.

Psychic Darkness: the Collective Pain

An encounter with fear is not a purely personal, private matter. It is communal and related to others. As John Donne says, 'No man is an island' and we are involved psychically with mankind, with others, both alive and those that have gone ahead of us. And with angelic minds as well as those of the diabolical kind. If we are unaware of this we cannot communicate effectively. The mere small talk that passes for communication is not effective. But we are all part of the universe and even the hairs on our head are all numbered.

We are in touch with all other souls psychically, and with the Holy Spirit; but the Spirit knocks at the door of those who pray, without entering unless invited. In this respect the Spirit is different from the kind of occult practitioner who seeks to enter and to dominate. For the psychic realm is morally neutral. This is why it needs purification by the Spirit of God. When this is not present all manner of murkiness can arise which is why the churches traditionally avoid the psychic. Yet the psychic realm can produce great prophecy as both the saints and the more current Charismatic Movement have demonstrated.

The darkness of this world can easily obtrude into the consciousness of psychically sensitive people. Such sensitivity is a painful gift, since it allows you no peace. Indeed it makes you more aware of the pain that affects the whole world. You are vulnerable, and it can lead you into the depths of hell. But if you can withstand this, it enables you to perceive the deepest troubles of others and to act as an agent of healing. You do not plan such encounters; if you did, the ego would be in charge and you would be subsumed by it. It seems that the true aspirant is progressively trained by the Holy Spirit. Jesus' agony in Gethsemane was surely comprised of the experience of all the sin of the world in a psychic sense, not solely an awareness of his impending death. Diabolic psychic awareness has been compared to sulphurous fumes – a psychic stench – that causes you to retch and threatens to pull you apart. It is said that in such moments an 'arrow' prayer of intensity can connect with the whole company of heaven. But the cup is not removed. It never is in the hard school of life. Those who have experienced this and come through it are effectively 'born again' into a greater understanding of reality. Many clearly find the stress and fear too much for them, and this may be the inner cause of some suicides. But for those who are able to live courageously a day at a time through this 'valley of the shadow of death' there is the ability to guide others through this process to the 'delectable mountains' that lie beyond.

The Heart of Suffering

The encounter of despair in the psychic realm is the ultimate that the seeker can experience. Only when we have confronted the ultimate in ourselves can we bring that hell to God. The knowledge of God however which results, is a glowing intense inner relationship. We can grow to a higher level of prayer. Not all approaches to God are through anguish or torment. We may aspire through our physical body, though the process may be long, and we have to accept the physical limitations placed upon us as we grow older. Yet in Isaiah's word 'by his scourging we are healed'. The problem of personal suffering will not be resolved until we pass beyond the ego-centred nature of our being.

All attempts at justifying God's ways will fail. We cannot relate the arbitrary nature of God to our concepts of justice and order. To the atheist this is of course no problem. But to most of us there is a yearning for a morally perfect world. Yet to evil there is no automatic pattern apart from some of the more obvious instances of cause and effect. There is no rational explanation for the fact of evil in the presence of a loving God. This is why spiritual souls are not especially impressed by the kind of teaching that promises rewards in the hereafter that reflect our deeds on earth. Obviously we should all work for the good in our daily lives but what is needed is a total inner change, and this comes only from God.

In addition to the necessary suffering of ageing, disease and death, there is the trial of long periods of imprisonment for one's religion or beliefs. When this hits us we are incredulous at first, for each of us believes we are special – which in one sense we are. Then we try a series of orthodox and alternative forms of relief, or in the case of persecution, perhaps undue influence. Then we experience revolt when we realise we cannot escape. Finally the religious person has to accept that God is at the centre of the problem, as He was just as much in ancient Jerusalem as in the 20th century Holocaust. Then we have to realise that the providence of God is far above the justice of mankind. The mystics know that the glory of God is far above good and evil.

Strength in Weakness

God seeks to change our wholly human nature into that which is divine. This change is a gradual and an inward one. Our ego has to be subservient and not dominant if we are to change. The real life is one focussed on God, which we do by focussing upon love. We have to put away the concerns of success, affluence, the good opinions of our fellows, and embrace a peace that passes all understanding. This peace is not inertia. It is a relationship with God. It is a strength that is given to the weak. It is the humility and confession of the tax gatherer as against the triumphalism of the Pharisee. Those who survived the death camps tended to be those who had this inner strength. But those survivors formed a spiritual elite. Most of us would flee as did the disciples of Jesus after his betrayal. This is why the person of the Virgin Mary is so great, since she merely accepted what God wished throughout, and was pure in heart. Suffering concentrates our attention on the one thing we need for our salvation: the Spirit of God.

Vicarious Suffering

Suffering is an essential ingredient of life and enables us to grow spiritually. As we grow, so we are able to take a greater knowledge and acceptance of reality and truth. Much of the love we experience in our daily lives has a selfish element within it. We give and we expect in return. We yearn for security. Not that this love is solely negative: it involves a learning and a broadening of our spirit. When we have passed through suffering we emerge wiser and better people; this is not true of the arrogant kind of believer who seeks to dominate rather than to benefit. Care and love are both needed. Care brings resources to the distressed. Love brings ourselves, without which care becomes impersonal and 'as cold as charity' in the modern, negative sense of the term.

The heart of the matter is that only one who has emerged from the dark pit of suffering is able to live no more in himself but in God. Agnostic and atheist philosophers will argue interminably about the meaning of life and existence or otherwise of God. Only those who have found a meaning will know without doubt the answer.

Mankind was created in order to raise up the mortal into immortality. To achieve this the master has to become the servant. This raising up is the real ministry of healing, which is closely related to the Sacrament of Baptism. An intimation of universal healing is given in the prayer discovered in Ravensbruck Concentration Camp wherein forgiveness is sought for those of ill will as well as for those of goodwill, so that the fruits of comradeship bought by the inmates might serve to bring about the forgiveness of the wicked.

A factor is that we ourselves have to want to be healed. God does not thrust healing upon us against our will. There are some who use morbid suffering as a way to avoid the challenges of life. And those seeking to heal another have to be free of sentimentality. Some people engaged in healing feel they pick up the diseased condition of their patient. This may be due to a psychic sensitivity. In itself it is neither good nor bad, though it can inflate the ego of the healer which can be dangerous. Jesus Himself had to learn obedience in the school of suffering, and then to die so that death was overcome in victory.

The Suffering in Relationships

We cannot escape from an awareness that we have fallen short of the high standards that we are capable of achieving. This is a measure of becoming aware of our sin. It is a paradox that is a part of our human condition, and is reflected in the recorded lives of most biblical figures, as well as in the corporate life of God's people. Our life is a mosaic of suffering and happiness, as is reflected in various ways within the Eastern as well as the Abrahamic faiths. However, God is in control. Suffering is the way of growth into Christhood, and in suffering we complement the work of Christ. Simone Weil wrote, 'The extreme greatness of Christianity lies in the fact that it does not seek a supernatural remedy for suffering but a supernatural use for it.' There is no growth without pain. Dramatic conversion and healing may punctuate our life, but in between there are long periods of apparent stagnation and relapse. These can be the more valuable times, for our inner feelings are poor guides to our spiritual growth.

We may be burdened by our peer group. Few of us can easily tolerate criticism from those with whom we associate. And then there is the burden of having betrayed someone, on purpose or by accident. This produces a kind of spiritual stench which has to be purified by our aligning ourselves with the one we have wronged, before we can progress further. The converse also applies if we ourselves have been wronged. Until we have accepted and forgiven we cannot progress. The agony of guilt and the fury of resentment have both to be conquered before the 'pearl of great price' becomes ours. Even when we are freed from sin, the consequences of our actions may pursue us over the years. Julian of Norwich was shown that 'sin is behovable' but that in the end all shall be well. Sin makes forgiveness possible.

Equanimity

We come through suffering changed and renewed. Our reward – the knowledge of God – outstrips any price that we have to pay. This is the lesson of the labourers in the vineyard, who were given the same reward no matter how long they had worked. And in the Parable of the

Prodigal Son it is the dutiful elder brother – possibly devoted to religion and piety – who has to suffer, not appreciating that he too had his father's bounty and goodwill all along the way. In an earthly context one hopes that the two brothers found reconciliation and contentment in each other, possibly by some positive act of the prodigal – an act to bring about equanimity.

In equanimity, also called 'Holy Indifference', one is in touch with God. We accept things as they are, once they have been brought to God in faith. The triumph over suffering is that we are brought into a situation where there is neither pain nor pleasure, but just the peace of God. Some people go into long-term retreats from the world to bring about this peace. But this itself can be precarious since a sudden return to the everyday stress can be unbalancing. The experienced retreat conductor will give the retreatants detailed instructions for a disciplined life to obviate this. In a state of equanimity we can appreciate what Julian of Norwich calls the courtesy of God. When we are truly attached to God we can see all of mankind as our brothers and sisters without hierarchy or degree. 'Thy will be done' allows us to pray as we should. An Islamic sage was asked 'Do you love God?' Answer 'Yes'. Question 'Do you hate the devil?' Answer 'My love of God leaves me no leisure to hate the devil.' Suffering gives us the probationary path to God.

Taking Up the Cross

Jesus was strict. To follow Him we must leave self behind, regardless of our own safety. We do not have to make martyrs of ourselves, and the Lord's Prayer asks that we be not led into temptation or trial. We are not expected to be imprudent, for this tends to be a mark of the ego and of exhibitionism. The cross we are called upon to bear is a defect in ourselves that has to be faced. It is a signpost on the way that we have to travel to become full human beings. It can be likened to the Star of David that all Jews had to wear in the Nazi regime. It is a sign of degradation and discrimination but also a badge of courage as perceived by those who understand these things. It requires our courage as well as self-acceptance.

A cross we have to bear is the pain of comparing ourselves unfavourably with others. We do not realise the many gifts we have, floating through much of everyday life like sleep-walkers. And then there is the burden of living with harmful childhood memories, some of which are in the field of psychotherapy or counselling. As our cross is held aloft, the memories of the past are healed. And as we perceive that our own sins are forgiven we become able to forgive those that have sinned against us.

Retribution, Suffering and Atonement

There has always been a strong perceived connection between misdeeds and consequent misfortune, both in the Old Testament and the Apocrypha. In Ancient Greece and in Buddhism and Hinduism there has been a teaching that our true selves pre-exist our births and that we progress after death into absorption into the Absolute. Some believe in reincarnation to make this possible. Whilst one must have the severest reservations about some of the extreme irrevocable justice teachings of orthodox religion, there is nonetheless a truth that profound spiritual knowledge can only be given to those who have led spiritual lives. It is arguably to our benefit that no final proof is available to us of life after death, but it is true that we need a continuance beyond this life to finish the processes of progression that on earth we have started. How much of our trials are direct results of our sin, as in the Eastern doctrine of 'karma'? It is true that a great many of our ills in old age are contributed to by a misspent youth in a medical sense.

There are two kinds of suffering: the retributive and the redemptive. Retributive suffering is the karma of the East. I have done wrong and I must pay the penalty. When we are awakened we perceive what we are doing and start to avoid the karma. Redemptive suffering is when we have passed through a presumption of cause and effect that causes outrage when it doesn't happen as we expect and feel is our due. We have reached an acceptance of things as they are. The fruit of this kind of suffering is that we emerge as re-created people, able to do God's work.

So how about the suffering of children, who are totally innocent? It is here that the prospect of existence before and after birth and death becomes attractive. Although unpalatable to many Christians who accept the Catholic purgatorial view of the afterlife, having lived but once, the Eastern traditions of rebirth can be a fertile area for consideration. Death as we understand it is surely not a once-for-all occurrence.

Nothing happens to us solely by chance, and the child born defective, no matter how agonising for the parents, may well have something to teach us all about love – the giving or the receiving. We have to work out our own salvation, but Christ redeems karma, just as the father of the Prodigal runs out to welcome back his errant son. In this way, cause and effect becomes supplanted by the laws of spiritual growth.

The Path to Wholeness

If suffering is the route to wholeness, should we not leave our suffering neighbours to their fate? This unwarrantable attitude does point, however, to the truth that an inappropriate removal of some containable hardship may not serve as well as it appears. Sometimes we have to approach unflinchingly the source of our suffering without fear, so that it does not continue to cause destruction.

So what is the essential ministry of healing, if not to cure? It is to sustain the afflicted. It includes a vast range of disciplines, not restricted to those with medical skills. We are all potential ministers of healing, a more apposite title than 'healer'.

Life has its checks and balances, and these have to be accepted. Only a complete change of our attitude can save the world. This change is contained in the one word 'love'. The 'Antichrist' to all this is not an overtly diabolical 'devil'. It is a pleasantly seductive leadership figure that bids us all live pleasant, uneventful and utterly self-centred affluent lives, full of welfare and institutionalised secularism that gradually takes over and usurps the place of God.

The way to wholeness is like peeling the skins off an onion progressively until 'the pearl of great price' within is revealed. There are no short cuts in our development into spiritual beings. One maxim we should all observe if we wish to progress is always to treat others as we should like them to treat us. There is however an intense pain of the soul which cannot easily be explained to others. Only those who know this path can help others who are upon it. Spiritual progress is obtained not by alleviation of suffering but by penetration – piercing the darkness. The best way to help a person in spiritual distress is to be with them constantly – in person, by telephone, or in any other way. It is our presence that can help, not anything we say or do. And prayer is an essential act: intercession for the one in distress, and even deeper intercession for those who have gone on and are in deeper distress in the afterlife.

Healing Prayer

There are as many ways of praying as there are people who pray. It is God's will that all should be healed, but healing prayer is of a different order from other prayer. Many healing ministers do not realise this. Healing prayer is to transfigure the person, not merely to relieve them of their malady. God knows what we pray for before we ask it. He leads us into a quiet place so that we can receive the Holy Spirit, so that prayer can be valid. Prayer of any validity starts with silence. 'Be still and know that I am God.' We need to be agents of love. We need to have the capacity to love God and to love our fellow human beings. Of course we should ask for alleviation of sickness but this is only a beginning. We also must be obedient to God's final word or response. It is also important to be aware of any contributory factor that we may have made towards giving rise to the malady.

It is important also to pray for the dead, especially those who may have led self-centred lives. In their next life they may be closer to us than to the communion of saints, and so more amenable to the help we may give. Some psychically sensitive people are more erudite than others in this sphere. We may get help from Christ but we have to pray for it.

Healing prayer begins with the one who prays. Our life must not be disordered if we are to pray for others. We have to remove the plank in our own eye before we can see clearly the speck in another person's eye. Another important but surprising element is a sense of humour, which aids perspective. It is said that the fool and the clown are divine symbols. 'The devil, the proud spirit, cannot endure to be mocked' in Bacon's words. And humour, especially of the self-deprecating kind, helps to keep our own ego in its place. There is lightness about true spirituality that brings us into communion with the angels and spirits of light. The ideal is that our lives should become a living prayer and a witness to God's grace.

8. Healing as Sacrament - The Sanctification of the World

Bishop Morris Maddocks, then Chairman of the Churches' Council for Health and Healing, wrote the following appraisal of Martin Israel's book on Healing, published in 1984: *'Dr Israel has written a short but masterly account of the principles of spiritual healing in the wider context of the sanctification of the world. He steers a balanced and orthodox course through the healing labyrinth, especially in regard to the psychic, which he rightly treats and about which he presents a sane view. I think this will be his most lasting – and ultimately significant – book to date.'*

In the prologue it is asserted that the ministry of healing is often disturbingly fragmented due to sectarian loyalties, each practitioner concentrating almost exclusively on their own territory. When our minds are broad enough to perceive healing as a sacrament of God's grace leading mankind to its proper place in the world, we can begin to grasp the meaning of the subject.

The Nature of Healing.

At its simplest, healing is the restoration of health to a part of the body that was previously diseased. The body has a remarkable capacity for doing this for itself, and the discipline of medicine can now shed much light upon how this is done. It can describe the chemistry, but has still a lot to learn about the fundamental factors that control healing. Beyond the biological and the physical there appears to be much that is related to the emotional and the mental. In addition to such factors as diet and occupation there is the matter of mental attitude. The human personality functions on at least four levels: the physical, the emotional, the rational, and a deeper centre of moral decision-making often called the soul. The soul is sometimes separated into the true or spiritual self and the ego by which we express ourselves. We are told to love God and to love our neighbour, which means that we have to employ all four functions of our personality.

The basis of healing is integration. This is centred on the soul, the true self. The state that precedes healing is disintegration, which may follow on from some emotional upheaval such as disappointment, betrayal or bereavement. Our emotional life is related to our body –

notably the digestion – and to the rational mind that tries to deal with each situation, and also to the soul. But even the most integrated person is liable to injury or infection. Our response to life is an individual matter. Some are subsumed by illness; others rise above it to a greater or lesser extent and may respond to the challenge of dealing with it to the benefit of their integration. Before scientific medicine had advanced to its present level, the doctor would rely upon the natural powers of healing and such spiritual support or 'giving relationship' as he could give, which often was effective.

When we are mobilised on behalf of someone about whom we care, psychic energy for healing can be released, for we are indeed members of one body. To mankind belongs the duty and the privilege of caring for the other inhabitants of our world, animal and vegetable, and yet we are predatory. One day we shall be free of these contradictions, and indeed the spiritualisation of all life is the true purpose of healing. All other healing is partial and incomplete even though it may restore the body. Effective healing brings about the harmonious balance of the individual, nothing less.

The Faith that Heals

The faith that heals does not demand an uncomprehending acceptance of theories, nor does it require submission to dominant people who claim special powers. Balance, order and reason are essential features that accompany the faith that accompanies spiritual healing. Faith is worlds apart from credulity. It is an open, self-giving acceptance of a purpose that guides us. When God hears our petitions they are not automatically granted, but if we offer ourselves, the Spirit will infuse us. Our healing may be slow but it is more likely to be complete.

When we are converted, our whole way of life changes, and to achieve healing we need faith. But the opposite of faith is not doubt. Indeed a rational, sound faith will often be laced with doubt, lest it become mere credulity. The real barriers to faith are arrogance and hostility, which is related to the sin of pride, that puts us beyond the reach of God. There are some people whose very virtue stands in the way of healing because they resent the ill-fortune that has assailed them. We have to be open to God's grace to be open to healing.

God cannot be bribed. If we make a covenant for our healing it will not work, and if it appears to do so, it is probably due to some other factor. Hostility is a bar to the healing power of God.

The person who is privileged to offer healing needs faith as much as the person receiving it. This is a trust in God, not in one's own abilities. Peace of mind, openness, service and a suspension of egoistic desires and judgemental thoughts are the bases of the faith to give healing to others. If we seek personal triumph we are excluded, and firmly though we may believe that God's will is to heal, the attitude or stance must always be, 'Thy will, not mine.' It is noticeable that little children and animals often respond well to healing whether by prayer of by the method of laying on of hands.

Faith is sometimes tested by rejection, and it calls for patience. Some of the miraculous healings in the Bible reflect this, as do they also reflect the faith of others in bringing about healing: Jairus, whose daughter was sick, and the Roman centurion interceding for his sick trooper. In healings, some of which may involve Near-Death Experience, the patients will enter a new life following their recovery.

Repentance and Healing

Faith is a prerequisite for the Holy Spirit to work within us, and a like openness in our deeper selves, bordering on the subconscious mind, is also necessary. Among the blocks to this are pride, hostility and resentment, but also there is guilt that clouds our peace of mind. This is the subjective response to sin. To some present day thinkers the very concept of sin is outmoded. Sinful behaviour is ascribed to a reaction to overbearing authority figures from childhood, and therefore excused. Another source of guilt is the reaction to having broken free from a peer group or some other conventionally acceptable life, and having ascribed to oneself a feeling of having betrayed the group. Then there is a third source of guilt through having mistreated others in one's present daily life. Personal sin needs to be acknowledged and confessed before we can rise beyond it. And those who have the power to assail others in mind and body are especially to be feared.

When our awareness is blocked by guilt we cannot face ourselves and our fellows. The act of confessing, and seeking the absolution that always follows, reconciles us to God. But this leaves resentment which is as destructive as guilt. The means of escape from this are threefold: a realisation of the residual benefits that one has, an appreciation that one's own life has been far from perfect, and recognition of the love and devotion of those round about. This last is of extra importance, especially if it involves someone to whom we can unburden ourselves in love. We should never be ashamed of our feelings however naked. We progress not by suppressing them but by transfiguring them.

Is disease the result of sin? Often there is no direct relationship, especially with children who can hardly be accounted sinful to that extent. But at the cosmic level there is probably a connection. Confession followed by absolution by a priest is a sacrament – an outward and visible sign of an inward and spiritual grace. It should be followed by a penance, and the most valuable penance for most of us is the service to others, especially to those we may have wronged. Once the innocent have mastered any resentment and accepted absolution their blamelessness is transfigured into forgiveness and love. No longer is justice sought or revenge but an aspiration to be instruments of forgiveness.

The Refashioning of the Will

There can be no healing until the sick person wants to be healed. The will of the afflicted person must be positively directed towards recovery. This takes us to the whole question of how free any of us are, and to what extent we are directed by our unconscious minds, as many professionals would have it. There is our upbringing, the social mores expected by our associates, and other powerful forces that dictate how we seek to act. It is from the point of truth in the depths of our personality that our authentic will emanates, and it is directed by the Holy Spirit if it is to reach its perfection.

Freedom necessitates choice. It determines whether we remain as we are or else progress in the service of God. And it has to be said that not all of our conditioning is harmful. We need training and discipline to operate in our worldly environment. Why should anyone not wish to be healed? Partly, it involves picking up where we left off, without the physical or emotional crutches of being an invalid. Health is ultimately in our own hands. Once we have given of ourselves to God we have to participate in prayer, service, and sharing with others.

Whatever views one may have about the personality being obsessed by outside psychic forces, it is wise to keep an open mind on the subject. Until a degree of wholeness has been achieved there is always the possibility that one malady may follow another. Moreover physical illness may be followed by emotional breakdown and by misfortune of one sort or another than might even assail a whole family. Acting on our own will, may not be able to move us out of the harmful rut in which we find ourselves. Our will needs to be incisive and clean in its action so that there can be a progressive opening up of the whole personality. The cause of a failed healing is often ambivalence in the attitude of the person wanting to be healed. If we put our hand to the plough and then look back we are not yet ready for the Kingdom of God. Healing requires the entry of the whole person into a new way of life, in which service to others replaces the seductive ease of the past. The essential need of mankind is commitment. In the person attaining integration there can only be one nature. Our lower and higher natures must be integrated with the will of God.

The Unobstructed Vision

Jesus heals a man blind from birth. 'Who sinned?' ask the disciples, 'This man or his parents?' 'Neither', replies Jesus, 'He was born blind so that God's power might be shown.' Jesus was brought into conflict with the authorities over this and other healings. The blind man attains spiritual enlightenment. The religious authorities sink deeper into spiritual darkness. There is judgement here, part of the mission of Jesus. Our inner vision is all too often blocked by cares and distractions. An imminent crisis overwhelms us, and our view of reality becomes distorted. We see in another person that which we project on to them. Only when we are liberated from our prejudice can we see them in a new light. Then we may encounter kindness and consideration where previously we had perceived coldness or disdain. There can be no healing till we see life truly.

We need the light of God to illuminate us in life's darkness. It gives us a warm glow of concern for the whole of creation. When we follow that light our life is more than just our own life, but the life of Christ within us. Vision brings us all to a confrontation with what is eternal in each passing moment. This enables us to concentrate upon that which is eternal. It does not necessarily mean abandoning our daily life for some special calling but rather to go about our business here and now spreading God's love. In George Herbert's words, 'Who sweeps a room as for Thy sake, makes that and the action fine!' When Jesus performed his three miracles of raising from the dead he brought all three from death to a new vision of life. When we follow Christ we forsake our previous narrow life and live for our neighbour. The measure of a truly spiritually healed person is the steady transformation so that we cease to live for ourselves alone but increasingly for others. Thus the intellectual giants in our society may remain spiritually blind but the humble soul who receives God's grace eagerly as a little child may attain the vision of eternity. And as the prophet Isaiah observed, 'A little child shall lead them.'

Deliverance from Evil

The tale is told of the man tormented by an evil spirit whose name is 'legion, for we are many'. In delivering the man from his demons, Jesus causes the evil spirits to be passed into a herd of pigs which then perish.

The mind is often occluded by visions or memories from the past, some of which emerge from the subconscious. They cast their shadow on the present moment. Every action brings its corresponding reaction, so that the rule is, 'Judge not that ye be not judged'. As we measure out to others so it will be measured out to us. Our minds may be a seething mass of unresolved guilt or conflicting emotion and it is from this that much evil comes. We covet in others what we lack in ourselves. We seek to overthrow those more successful than ourselves. Within each of us there is the potentiality to be one with the crowd that jeered hideously at Calvary, which is matched in each generation by those who persecute unfashionable minorities with barbaric glee.

The origin of evil is an enigma. It may be merely an absence of good, or else a display of ignorance, though this seems a little glib. It seems to have a collective origin that may stem from abuse of the freewill granted us by Creation. When we set ourselves up separately apart from others, rivalry and hostility take over until we realise that our own wellbeing depends upon those around us.

Evil cannot be spirited away merely by rationalisation or by giving it a psychological name. Eventually the evil tendency has to be isolated and purged, and then redeemed. It has two aspects: the personal evil and that which infects society as a whole, which especially affects the vulnerable and those with psychic sensitivity. Our defence is to live an upright life and it can be protective to belong to a worshipping community. Deliverance from evil is essentially a labour of love – seeing the other person as infinitely valuable and being prepared to sacrifice for them.

Love is not the same as sentiment. It is a direct fearless confrontation with the other person as they are. Then comes judgement, which is best undertaken by the person themselves, perhaps in consultation with whoever is ministering healing. Evil tendencies have to be uncovered, but preferably by loving insight from the healing minister, and it is here that counselling and healing may converge. Once the evil has been acknowledged it must be offered to God in prayer; Jesus may be invoked depending upon the temperament of the sinner. The healing minister must share in the burden, helping to relieve from the outer darkness of realisation. In some cases the laying on of hands may help. Confession may help, not necessarily to a priest but to someone loving who may be trusted and who may intercede for the troubled person. Needless to say the confessor must exercise the utmost discretion, comparable to that of a doctor. No one should enter the healing ministry unless they have achieved the necessary experience and discretion never to become inappropriately entangled in a patient's difficulties.

Love is quiet and effective in healing. It cannot force itself upon anyone. It must await the invitation, but when summoned it will take control and will not let go. Obliging the beloved to face truths is essentially part of the process of deliverance from evil.

There is, however, one aspect of evil that was commonly understood in Jesus' time but much less so today. This is the kind of psychic disturbance that can emanate from mischievous entities the other side of death, which may especially prey upon the immature and mentally disturbed. Often the cause of the trouble is indeed within the subject themselves, but there are occasions when an outside influence appears to be at work. This needs specialist attention from someone with developed psychic sensitivity. It may be an innate gift they have, or else one acquired by experience – often the better way. Many with natural healing gifts come into this category, and to remain whole in their specialised work they need to live a life of prayer, worship, and work for others. The humanistic or materialistic follower of religion tends to scoff at all this. Such people also have difficulty in believing in a meaningful conscious life after the death of the physical body, which of course is consistent. The enthusiastic exorcist on the other hand tends to see all difficulties as the fruits of demonic attack. The essential spiritual practitioner exercises judgement, and re-aligns the will so that we cease to do evil and start to do good. So the sinner is loved and the sin banished. In the ministry of deliverance the invading entity is called out in the name of the Trinity but is not left to perish, but is re-directed. Prayer should always follow a deliverance, since it is easier to dislodge a source of evil than to replace it with peace and love.

Healing is often viewed as something given to the afflicted from outside. This is just the initial phase. It needs to be followed by the strengthening of the person from within themselves. And it needs to be stated that whether or not a malady involves evil infestation from outside, there is always personal responsibility, which each of us has to accept. The grace of God initiates the healing work once the will to be healed is present – akin to the 'right mindfulness' that we all need, so stressed by the Buddha six hundred years before the birth of Christ.

The Sacraments in Healing

Every object in our lives is potentially a sacrament – an outward sign of a spiritual reality. Dame Julian of Norwich is shown the tiniest thing, the size of a hazelnut. She asks what it is, and is told that it is all that is made. She marvels that it might survive. She is told that it shall last forever because God loves it, and it has three properties: God made it, God loves it, and God keeps it. Hence the divine essence is in all created things. The intrinsic holiness that is in all matter depends upon the human touch for its sanctity to be made clear in the world. Here the priesthood of the whole of mankind becomes manifest. Whatever is handled with reverence in the name of God is consecrated to His use and becomes an object of blessing. Without ceasing to be itself it also finds its eternal meaning. No work is intrinsically menial in God's sight: even the cleaning of a toilet can be as close to God's service as the act of consecration in the Eucharist. The holiness of all matter was proclaimed when the Word became fully flesh and dwelt among us.

The products of the earth can be summarised in the bread we need to sustain us each day and the wine that restores us after a day's toil. In the totally unredeemed person that is all they are, and they may even lead to gluttony. It is the Holy Spirit infusing the substance of the world that makes them holy. This holiness is made real by the humans who consecrate themselves and all that they use to God's service. The sacraments of the Church remind us that Christ has given of himself for the creation of all material, and when it is blessed in His name, He is there with us as well as in the physical object itself, which then bears a healing and restoring property. Thus the Eucharist becomes the principal healing sacrament of the Church, though all that we eat and drink have a sacramental quality when consumed with reverence and thanksgiving.

Baptism is the initial healing sacrament, bringing us symbolically through death into the community of believers. It is completed in the Eucharist. The other great healing sacrament is Holy Unction, the anointing of the sick person with consecrated oil. Oil is enriching, lubricating and soothing. From ancient times it has been used to make a king or priest a holy person, anointed of God. It has also been used to anoint the sick, and until recent times this was normally restricted to the dying, hence the term 'Extreme Unction'. Nowadays it is frequently used as a healing medium for all sick people. If possible there should first be a time to counsel, ending with confession and absolution and followed by prayer; of necessity this is curtailed in the case of the desperately ill.

In the sacramental approach to healing a part of the minister's own body is added to the natural elements – the use of human hands. The sacramental elements are prepared by human hands in the first instance and are prepared on the altar by whosoever is presiding. St Teresa of Avila reminds us that Christ has no body now on earth but our body, and no hands nor feet but ours. Indeed the body given in service is itself a mighty sacrament. In fact the whole world is a sacrament if only we had eyes to see. The Church is a sacrament as the Mystical Body of Christ, as are all the specific sacramental observances that we have mentioned. They help us to remember that God is never far from us even though times are hard. When we have departed from his world we shall see the full sacramental nature of the universe. This links the seen to the unseen, until there will ultimately be but one sacrament: the universe united with God.

Prayer and Healing

Prayer is at the heart of healing. All healing comes to us by the grace of God. Although we think that it is we who do the praying, it is God the Holy Spirit who is the foundation of our prayers – 'the ground of our beseeching' as Dame Julian of Norwich puts it. Prayer is as essential to our souls as breathing is to our physical bodies. Our praying may start with a list of wants, and then may extend to confession. When we pray for help we are not telling God anything He does not already know. But He does not see as mankind sees. God judges by the heart.

What is God's position as regards healing? He surely wills wholeness for all His creatures but there is still the problem of evil, and disease and suffering may sometimes be necessary to attain wholeness. Our prayers may start with a list of wants and then nothing happens. If we persist, however, a deeper knowledge of God finally emerges, and we learn to remove our ego from the centre of concern. To desire a return to health to live as a better servant would seem to be entirely praiseworthy, but there may be undercurrents that distort the picture and delay healing. The essence of true discipleship to Christ is obedience to the Father and love of neighbour, who is everyone in our vicinity. In healing prayer there are two pitfalls: an over-concern with bodily cure and an under-concern. A true healing raises the person to a higher level of integration, which can be hard to achieve whilst we are imprisoned in bodily concerns.

Sometimes a startling bodily cure is the means whereby a previously spiritually dead person comes to life. Nor need this healing be charismatic – it may be the result of orthodox medical treatment. It may also be that someone undergoing major surgery will experience a spiritual renewal or a surge in strength or faith. The basis of prayer here should not be for rapid physical recovery but simply that the Spirit of God should infuse the patient with renewed life and purpose. The end is God's will, not ours. Activism – the feeling that we have to do something – can be the bane of human endeavour, since it leads to self-justification and so to dissatisfaction. Activity, on the other hand, is the way of the Spirit. It begins with prayer and leads on to calm assessment and so to purposeful action.

In healing prayer there is the danger that we feel ashamed at our impotence, and that if we were truly spiritual we could rise above bodily constraints and commune with the divine. This can be a dangerous Gnostic attitude that exalts the spirit and denigrates the body. We have to embrace both body and spirit to bring about a healing that lasts. It includes an acceptance of adversity that recognises that all things work for the best for those who love God. The person who prays is the sacrament of the new race of people who will know God in the depths of their being.

The Gift of Healing

The gift of healing comes from God through the Holy Spirit. In the healing ministry we need an openness to God and a deep concern for our fellow human beings. We must be able to accept ourselves as we are, in order to forget ourselves in the service of God and of others. It is the gift of being able rapidly to make deep soul-relationships, and if we have this gift we shall be the focus of healing powers wherever we go. We shall not need to display ourselves. The basis of our gift is prayer – not to make our gift known, but to be kept aware of God's will in each situation.

In true healing there is no glamour – only unmitigated service. A person serving in a shop or a supermarket can be a minister of healing when they flow out in concern to a customer, giving their whole attention to meeting the customer's needs. The same applies to any of us when we help a stranger in difficulty, and our healing may greatly surpass the intrinsic or apparent value of the service performed.

It cannot be over-emphasised that the essence of healing is an attitude of quiet, unassuming hope that emanates from one who is shriven of selfish desires, possibly having learnt through adversity. There is a difference between a virtuous person and a holy person. The virtuous person, though well-meaning and unexceptionable in themselves, will tend to judge others by their own high standards. The holy person, on the other hand, brings God closer to all who come into contact with them – a basic but pervasive humility. It is an attitude of complete harmlessness and love. A healing gift is indeed a gift from God, and if we have it, we have a great privilege to be used to His honour. Jesus never took credit for his powers, but always gave thanks to God. But there are responsibilities. We need ourselves to be healthy in mind, body and soul in order to do our work effectively. And we must accept the limits of our own health and strength and know when to say 'no'. The patient or person seeking healing should be instructed about true faith and an openness to God, so that the healing ministry is also a teaching ministry. The secret is constructive thinking and living – when there is balance between body and soul, mind and heart.

Some healers with a spiritualistic turn of mind believe that discarnate spirits who have gone on take a part in the healing ministry, and they may turn to spirit guides. These need not be dismissed out of hand, since we know too little about the spirit world. However it is right that our attention should be lifted up to God in prayer rather than diverted to psychic entities. The most serious criticism of psychic communication in general is the trivial nature of so much of it, added to which is the danger of mischievous entities becoming involved and clouding the situation.

A similar criticism can be true in some churches where healing services are part of the regular liturgy. The mere laying on of hands at the altar is not enough. It must be accompanied by authoritative teaching and also counselling. Alternative as well as scientific medicine may have a place in a holistic approach to healing, provided there is also mature discernment: the wisdom of the serpent and the harmlessness of the dove.

Among the dangers of the healing ministry is the tendency to dominate the lives of the patients, in a zeal to prove the ways of God by results. If healing fails, we conclude that it must therefore be due to lack of faith or else unacknowledged guilt. In such heartless judgements it is the faith of the healer that is to be questioned. We should not practise in the healing ministry until we ourselves are sufficiently balanced and integrated to be able to avoid such aberrations. Likewise there should never be a charge for our services, though spontaneous gifts may themselves be therapeutic. It is always preferable that we should earn our living other than by the use of spiritual gifts, if at all possible, and in any case that a part of each day is devoted to other than healing situations, to keep ourselves balanced and in perspective.

Healing ministry is a gift of love to all who will receive it.

The Problem of the Unhealed

No account of the healing ministry is complete and authentic unless it deals with the painful and pertinent question of those who apparently fail to be healed. These would seem to be a significant proportion of those whom scientific medicine has failed to cure and who have turned to seek spiritual help. It is an unfortunate facet that orthodox doctors tend always to remember their failures whereas unorthodox practitioners just remember and broadcast their successes. Indeed we still look for the kind of controlled trials in alternative treatments that are the norm in drug and orthodox forms of treatment. Anecdotes of success are not an acceptable response. Even when we sift out those people who could be simplistically dismissed as having had no religion at all and thus no call upon God to heal them, we are still left with a considerable number of earnest sufferers who have failed to respond to the full ministry of healing. They are a continuing source of embarrassment to those dedicated agencies of healing that pride themselves on a near perfect record of service to all who approach them. Is God's power or His love to be called into question?

The answer to this problem appears to lie in the prevalence of hatred and sin. We are all parts of one body, and even the concept of a personal healing can be seen as self-centred unless it is perceived in the context of the resurrection of the whole world. It is said that no saint can be in heaven as long as one soul remains in hell, and Pascal observed that Christ will be in agony until the end of the world. As prophesied in Isaiah 53, 'with his stripes we are healed'. The wounds of those who learned to forgive their persecutors even as they were hounded to death are in this respect added to those of their protectors who died in faithfulness to the truth.

This means that pain has its own contribution to make, and we have to assimilate this as part of our growth. None of us is going to survive in our present form. Death is the gateway to a fuller life. What is important in this life is that we grow closer to one another in understanding. We live in the world of the Unjust Steward where we can be justified by the good turns we do for our fellows, no matter how impure our motives may be. It is God's will that we shall be healed, but we too have to play our part. In Psalm 116 it is said, 'A precious thing in the sight of the Lord is the death of those who die faithful to Him.' To those who have passed the test of suffering is the privilege of helping others in this life or the next. Within the Communion of Saints we communicate with them and they with us. And to quote Dame Julian of Norwich, in the end all shall be well.

It is our privilege 'in the days of our youth' to serve God in the fullness of health and strength. Then as we grow infirm we have the opportunity to suffer with Christ and to grow in the school of suffering.

The Resurrection of the Body

The purpose of our being alive is to make real the divine spark within us so that we come to share in the very being of God. This requires that we progress from our very necessary physical body to a spiritual body, which we are building even as we live. The purpose of spiritual healing is to open up our personality to the full impact of the Holy Spirit. To quote Isaiah, it is to bring good news to the humble, bind up the broken-hearted, proclaim liberty to captives, release prisoners, proclaim a year of the Lord's favour, and comfort the mourner.

All life is punctuated by little deaths, where our certainties are disrupted and we are led to adopt new understandings. Ultimately we come to realise that we own nothing, and our apparent possessions are to help us grow into more responsible people. As we have become at the end of this life, so shall we start in the next, but without a physical body in which to hide our baser emotions. There is a time in the healing process when we have to say 'thy will be done' whether we are terminally ill, or congenitally sick. We are only complete when we have commended our spirit into God's hands.

There is much we do not know about our physical universe and about which we can only conjecture. St Paul speaks of death being swallowed up in victory, and perishable things being raised up imperishable, and this may happen on a cosmic scale as well as in personal terms, in ways we can only imagine with difficulty. We have to learn the supreme lesson of loving our enemies. Love combats evil with the intent of saving those under its thrall. And this certainly means loving our neighbour. Christ is in our neighbour and so is our neighbour, and also our friend, which should encourage us. Ultimately the healing of physical and mental disorder precedes the complete transformation of the human personality into something of the nature of God.

9. Happiness that Lasts

This book, published in 1999, was among the last that Dr Martin Israel wrote. It belongs to the period following the end of his ministry as Priest-in-Charge at Holy Trinity Church, South Kensington, when he had been forced into retirement by a collapse in his health and a near-death experience, which he describes. Dedicated to his friend Rupert Cordle, who looked after his affairs during the last years of his life, he meditates upon the true values in life. The book opens with a quotation from William Blake:

'Tyger Tyger, burning bright, In the forests of the night, What immortal hand or eye, Dare frame thy fearful symmetry?'

Happiness is what we all need. If everyone were happy there would be no ill will, because all of us would be content. So what makes us happy? Many would put money top of the list, coupled with enough power to control our own lives (and discreetly to control the lives of others too). Those with more experience would rank health as the most important facet, and few could disagree. If we were still more profound we might list friendship as an essential, which may be sexual or platonic, and which might have family associations. And again others might put love as the one thing necessary, the snag being that this can be interpreted in a range from beneficent concern for all people right down to mere selfish lust.

How is true love achieved? It is an act of the will, but not of the selfish will so much as the will of God. Paradoxically this may involve a descent into darkness because as long as we are taken up with ourselves, God is occluded from our sight. Yet if we can persevere through the darkness we shall experience joy and the warmth of happiness. For the ordinary person this progression is not particularly easy or pleasant; but it is authentic. The greatest story of suffering as a precursor to happiness is of course the story of Jesus Christ, followed by the development of a degree of civilisation that has been achieved by those who claim to follow his path.

None of these earlier prerequisites to happiness are illusory, but they tend to be transitory. Even the absence of good health can result in a disablement that leads to inner peace.

The Darkness inherent in life

Nothing changes our attitude to life more than sudden dramatic adversity. Black may seem like white. Tragedy may open us out into a world of enormous potentiality. Recently there has been much literature on the subject of life and death, and the near-death experience. In it, the person returns to awareness and recounts what happened during a period of bliss. *(Martin Israel's own NDE, which lasted some eight months, is recounted in detail within this chapter on 'Darkness'. We describe it in outline within an earlier chapter 'Martin Israel – A Biography', and it is therefore not dealt with here).*

The illusion of wealth

Most people think that having more money would make them happy. It is certainly true that money can bring security and that poverty can bring unhappiness and we would be foolish to deny it. This appears to deny one principle of the monastic life that vows to live in poverty, chastity and obedience. Yet monks and nuns are not unhappy, so are they failing the religious life? Certainly not, for the religious have sufficient means for survival and for their immediate needs, and – though without possessions – they have sufficient leisure to be detached from worldly concerns and to concentrate upon prayer.

So does much money make us happy? Experience suggests that few millionaires are exceptionally happy, especially those whose wealth has been inherited and who may have followed a rigid or conventional form of upbringing which may have been far from elevating. The crux of the matter is that money is no guide to the good life or its enjoyment. Whilst no balanced person would deny the importance of substance in one's life, when it becomes the ruling passion it assumes a dictatorial power and determines how and with whom we live. This does not necessarily bring happiness.

Accumulation of wealth brings with it a capitalist quality, and this divides people into strata of society. It is curious that what was communism in Eastern Europe, with all its manifest evils, has now been replaced by a most grasping kind of capitalism in which relatively few families possess most of the wealth. Both forms of society are equally unsatisfactory, and all of this goes to show how superficial is contentment based upon wealth, when it is regarded as the sum total of the good life. It may form part of the foundation, but we dwell uneasily in its shadow. A tale is told of a man who unexpectedly inherited a fortune. Unused to it, he spent wildly among influential associates until owing to the deceit of others, he lost a good deal. Only then did he begin to discover the satisfaction of living for others and in accordance with his conscience, free from the necessity of following the opinion of other people.

Wealth that could lead to happiness

There is an ambivalence in wealth. It itself it does not bring happiness, but an absence of wealth does not necessarily bring unhappiness, though there is the obvious tendency. As previously suggested, inherited wealth can bring a kind of incarceration, though acquired wealth from a modest base can bring satisfaction.

It seems that the things on this earth which have material value can teach us responsibility but also we learn the temporary nature of such things. This does not mean that wealth is trivial, but that its importance is not permanent. Paradoxically the poor, who have never had very much, are nearer a state of freedom from concern than the wealthy, who are often bowed down with concern for looking after what they have.

Another aspect of affluence is that the more we have, the less meaning it has for us. This is particularly true for the children of rich parents. Whilst some may inherit the drive of their creative parents, others will while away their lives and opportunities in ways that do not yield results. Hence the proverb 'clogs to clogs in three generations'.

Money can be a spur to us to engage in useful activity, but until society ceases to judge people by the measure of their wealth, there will be unhappiness and discontent. In my own life I have been at my happiest when serving others in the fields of healing, counselling and the ministry of deliverance, for which I have never received payment. It has been rewarding to make others happy, especially those who have shared my own experience of low self-esteem. The work that I was called to do involved joining the priesthood and living in a way that could not bring about material gain or high reputation, and but for this it would have been very hard to proceed effectively. My material wealth developed quite independently through sound investment which enabled me to live in retirement with the care that I had begun to need.

To help others in the way I have described, one has to be strong. This is because those in trouble inevitably tend to lean upon us. Such leaning, though natural, is undesirable because neither party is left free to develop their own essential independence and self-reliance.

To help others in these specialised ways we should never seek any kind of acknowledgement, as Jesus' attitude in this respect makes clear. When everyone in the world has reached the state of patience and dedication to follow this way of life, we shall all be on the way to becoming complete human beings. We shall have no need of saints because each of us is doing our part, and wealth is no longer an issue because it can be shared.

The Place of Power

How can we become powerful without being a menace to others? The answer is to know ourselves. The more self-knowledge we have, the better we are able to control our own excesses. Then we can begin to listen to others rather than to try and dictate to them.

Most of us like helping others but we have to beware, so long as within us there is a need to dominate. Alas the 'Lady Bountiful' within us may be well-meaning but in time tends to undermine any good that we feel we are doing. Gratitude may soon turn to rejection as we become more and more inappropriately involved in matters that are not our business. The most valuable giving is the giving of the whole person, and those who give secretly may be rewarded openly.

Worldly power is attractive because of the social position it may give us. At one time it was aligned with wealth, though with the reversal of roles that has accompanied much well-meant philanthropy much of this has been turned upside-down. The Welfare State has been an excellent and necessary thing in itself, but when the rights of the poor, without responsibility, become a political issue then problems arise.

Allied to the social status granted by power is the growth in personal status. Richelieu wrote, 'The pen is mightier than the sword' which suggests that the power of the mind to influence is the really important agent of powerful action. Upon the negative side, the influence of propaganda and the rise of Adolf Hitler demonstrate the truth of this. Yet on the positive side, the power of fragile works of art, literature and poetry to inspire can result in changing the lives of many people. The Parable of the Talents teaches us the importance of using the gifts we have, and not burying them in the ground. For the truth is that what we have is not ours; we are guardians of it, to use for the best advantage of humanity before we pass on.

Power is at its best when it is given of itself freely to others. If I pride myself unduly with it, that pride will ultimately pass down to others. Paradoxically there can be power in weakness as St Paul teaches. And we should seek to love our neighbour as ourselves.

Self-knowledge is a lifelong process. It begins in childhood when we necessarily have a self-oriented view of the world and of ourselves. Then we learn that others have their own concerns and react differently to us. Gradually we develop from feeling that we are the centre of the universe to a realisation that we are but an infinitely small part of things. Then we may come to a moment of full self-knowledge when some event or challenge reveals our true selves. At this point we also begin truly to know the love of God.

Health and Happiness

If there is one single thing that would seem to determine our happiness, it is of course good health. We take this for granted until we do not have it, and then we tend to grumble. As we grow older we inevitably come to terms with less robust health, and yet surprisingly the older we get the more we become reconciled to the age we have reached. And today we can all expect to live longer. For some the state retirement age is the time to put one's feet up and relax. For others it is the occasion to re-launch themselves into a new burst of activity that may have been denied them when they were tied to the world of work.

Health is often the essential ingredient. So does that mean that the individual condemned to chronic ill-health is destined to be miserable? This depends upon their response, and whether they hide behind their disability or else use it as a spur to greater effort. The composer Beethoven is surely an example of one who triumphed over adversity, suffering deafness – surely the cruellest of fates for a composer. Despite early depression he fought back with greater endeavour, communicating in writing when he could no longer hear what was said to him, and producing some of his best work at the end of his life.

Modern medicine now takes better care of us, but we still have to face ultimate decay and death. Despite the 'near-death experience' which can be encouraging, no one in this life can know with certainty what the next life will be like. What we are surely expected to do is to live this life to the best of our ability in the present moment. 'Sufficient unto the day is the evil thereof'.

Health is not solely a personal matter. Only when people in general are satisfied with their living conditions can the corporate life be healthy. And this raises issues of the structure of society, of capitalism and socialism. Only when we ourselves have hit the bottom and bounced back can we truly identify with those who do not have enough. Then can we play our part in healing the ills of society.

Many creative brains other than that of Beethoven have reached heights of achievement despite poor health or short lives. When we can drive ourselves against the odds and bring about what we have been destined to do, then greatness can be revealed within us all. The greatness of a person lies in their being true to themselves.

So how do we attain health? A healthy mind surely plays its part, since it gives us a healthy purpose. This contributes to a healthy body. There are many external as well as internal pressures that contribute to our wellbeing or militate against it. 'No man is an island' and we are all involved in mankind as a whole.

And what about those who can see no point in anything that does not contribute to their own personal welfare or advantage? It is useless to preach to them (and indeed preaching in general has its limitations.) Such people have to learn their inadequacy by personal experience.

'Why did it happen to me?' is a question we all may ask. The answer is often because there was a lesson we had to learn. When we have learnt that we amount to nothing, then we can begin to play our important part in the scheme of things. This understanding puts the perplexities of health into perspective – especially those puzzles that arise from inherited disease. Our life on earth is illuminated as a result of Divine inspiration which leads us towards immortality.

Friendship and Happiness

When we are young our friendships tend to be superficial. Then when we are in hardship our friendships deepen, though the numbers tend to drop off. A test of true friendship is the capacity to support our friend even to our own disadvantage. And if it is to be real, the friendship must have permanence. We may have 'emotional chemistry' that draws us together quite apart from political, social or other affiliation. There is usually a sexual element in friendship, though this does not prevent platonic friendships between man and woman. When there is a strong physical element this may progress to conjugal love. Paradoxically one can be drawn to another physically without being drawn emotionally.

Friends may be joined together by a variety of bonds. A family ideally ought to be a group of friends, though anyone who has done family counselling knows that a family can become a little monster. We do not necessarily agree with our friends on everything, though a test of friendship will be how we can come through disagreements to a deeper understanding. A friend will never let you down, yet will have their own interests and commitments which they will pursue independently.

The friendships that Jesus Christ did – and did not – have can form an interesting study. Especially there is His relationship with Judas Iscariot. What was it that led to such a betrayal and yet led on to the fulfilment of the Resurrection?

Self-sacrifice is a keynote of true friendship. When a friend is in trouble we hasten to help if we can. One religious group, the Quakers, describe themselves as a Society of Friends, and their record has been exceptional in social reform and the abolition of slavery for example.

Within families the element of friendship is essential, especially to temper the degree of discipline that is often necessary to hold things together. Discipline is indeed an essential part of happiness, and the human problem is to strike the middle way, between too much control on the one hand and excessive licence on the other in which every aberration is regarded as acceptable.

The opposite of friendship is loneliness, which can be depressing. The solitude can be hard to bear. There are two factors which influence this: the stance of the person themselves, and the society in which they find themselves. Some of us are naturally gregarious and make friends easily. The negative side of this is that many of these friendships are superficial. The introvert on the other hand finds social contact difficult. This is made harder to bear when there is religious or political segregation. Yet if we can suffer this and survive we may become stronger and better adjusted people. Hence loneliness may be considered as the opposite of friendliness rather than of friendship.

Another social dimension is popularity. Whilst superficially linked to friendship this is fundamentally different. Whilst friendship tends to develop through experience, popularity is fundamentally fickle and may give the illusion of relationships that are largely without substance. As Jesus said, 'Alas for you when all speak well of you, because that is how their fathers treated the false prophets'.

Another aspect of true friendship is the nature of loyalty. This should not be limited to individuals. Whatever you do, if you are my friend, I will not desert you. But if you fall out with another, this does not mean that I must fall out with them as well, in order to be loyal. Friends do not compromise one another's integrity. Among the great friendships in the Bible are those between David and Jonathan, and the intense relationship with Saul, leading to David's lament in 2 Samuel in the Old Testament. Friendship in the New Testament is assumed rather than described. Indeed it is doubtful to what extent religious zeal actually encourages friendship as such. All too often it can lead to inflexibility and hatred.

Love and Friendship

Love is usually described as an intense emotional attachment between two people, often including the physical. Especially it is the attachment between two married people. Human love has a quality that sets it apart from noble friendship. But then we have Christ's commandment 'Love one another, as I have loved you.' To this St John adds the definition of the greatest love: that someone should lay down their life for their friends. And then there are the statements of St Paul. Love surpasses any language, either of men or of angels. It also surpasses prophecy, truth, and even faith. Giving all that we have is of no account if we have not love in our hearts. 'Cold as charity' is a saying that illustrates the point that giving on its own is beside the point.

Love will last forever. That is another dimension of love. When we love a person we know them, and this requires self-knowledge also. This is necessary so that we can distinguish pure love, which is giving, and selfish desire, which is seeking for oneself. The modern age tends to disregard such distinctions, and insufficient attention is paid to the need for self-control. In present times the whole basis of morality is the subject of much debate, especially in the matter of sexual conduct, and most of us could do worse than remain silent rather than become judgemental.

Then there is married love, which as a natural celibate myself there is only so much that I should say, save what I have observed as a counsellor. The key difference between marriage and most other friendship relationships is that of living under one roof. Partners are bound spiritually and also legally. This can be an intense test of love. Friends can and often do spend time apart. Spouses rarely have this latitude, for a variety of reasons connected with responsibilities. Marriage is not a state in which people live happily ever after. There is bound to be discord as each partner works out their own salvation. The great lesson that marriage teaches is tolerance, and that is why divorce can be so regrettable unless there really is no other way. Another essential of marriage is self-control, despite which many partners do have 'affairs'. It is usually better if these can be encompassed within the marriage, rather than accepted as 'the unacceptable' that must therefore lead to permanent separation. This is especially so where children are involved – whose interests should be a burning issue. A physical relationship within a marriage, though desirable, is not an essential especially where love persists.

Another aspect of life is the extreme undesirability of abortion. This can leave behind it all manner of distress, mental and physical.

What of the marriage that has become humdrum but respectable until one partner meets the light of their life – a 'Brief Encounter' as it were? My own observation, free of any prejudice, is that in most cases the marriage should continue if it possibly can. Married life is not simply a pleasure cruise through the rest of one's life. It is a journey of self-development in which each partner must progress. We are most real when we forget ourselves and give to others. Life is our most precious gift and we need to use it to the best advantage for mankind.

Society has always had its marginalised people, and in our generation this has included gays and lesbians. Nowadays there is a much kinder and more informed attitude. Same-sex love is obviously not the commonest form of love, but it is surely not anyone else's business to pry into the sexual lives of their fellows. This love is clearly a devotion that deserves to be accepted as 'love' and as such is of the Divine. One's private prejudices are clearly one's own affair, but my own belief is that sexual orientation is in most cases determined from birth, and is part of one's destiny.

A celibate is one who has always been single or who has embraced the single state deliberately. This may be imposed physically or else, as in my own case, it may be as natural as one of the sexual orientations albeit promoted by aspects of my upbringing. Can a celibate love? Celibacy can be the precursor to monumental selfishness, but it is also the way to supreme giving. The two greatest spiritual teachers, Jesus Christ and Gautama Buddha, did their work in the celibate state. Natural celibacy is a grace, though it may bring loneliness. Yet life itself brings loneliness especially with old age, which in the modern age can regrettably lead to institutional living. Provided one avoids the trap of self-centredness, celibacy enables one to give more fully, since there is not the prior and quite proper claim of one's family to be cared about.

What about love on a larger scale? 'I vow to thee my country' as the poem begins. This is the love that embraces many, and includes patriotism. That is fine provided it is extended to a concern and love for other nations as well. One thinks of the Europe of the last century, and also South Africa, and of the special devotion of individuals such as Bishop Trevor Huddleston and Archbishop Desmond Tutu. It is obvious that love allows these amazing sequences of events and emergence of special people, and one must pray that such instances continue to thrive in the future.

Spirituality and Religion

It is clear that the things of this world do not ultimately satisfy the soul, even when possessed to the full. But what is the soul? It is an inner awareness of what ultimately we all need, though we may not acknowledge it. It is not the same as morality, which literally means 'the customs of the people' whatever these may be at the relevant times and in the relevant places. (Capital punishment is now considered immoral in Europe but it's very much alive in USA.)

The more secure we are in ourselves the easier it is to avoid judging others. The Parable of the Pharisee and the Publican, followed by the story of Jesus 'suffering the little children' to come to Him, illustrates the difference between religion and spirituality. The essential quality of spirituality is the person's innate yearning for the Divine, which we call God. Yet God is within us. Many of the mystics teach that whatever we say about God is wrong. And as Robert Browning says, 'Truth is within us'. Spirituality involves following the Middle Way, as the Buddha taught, and avoiding extremes.

Spirituality involves self-control, self-knowledge and self-abasement. It is not an easy path to follow because it takes us away from the diversions of the world. And it does not bring us superficial happiness. But no one on the path to God thinks on those lines. There is a pearl of great price that when found brings joy. I began my life as a mystic when a child. I would frequently converse with God. The writer of the book, *'Mister God, this is Anna'* was also a mystic like me and though we respect religion there is a quality of the universal within all of us that one cannot subscribe solely and absolutely to the form of any one creed. And although the spiritual gift is inborn, it grows only through adversity.

The main value of religion is that it raises us, if we are of good intent, to a vision of what we might be if we were to behave like true children of God. It gives us a framework within which confession and true repentance can precede meaningful forgiveness – not just a comfortable way of escape for us. And good religion brings us to understand the true love of God, without the irrelevance of the 'very religious' kind of person that is apt to appear superior and to 'wrong-foot' us because of their attitude. When we worship God in the right way we forget self, and in that way we approach God like a little child.

Good religion sets us in the right direction, though the humble supplicant can be nearer the truth than many assured professing religionists. Unfortunately we tend to recognise this only after we have suffered in the process, and rid ourselves of the tendencies to judge others and to glory in their downfall.

Religion can also help us to pray. We do not need religion for this purpose but it gives us the framework and sets up the discipline. Prayer is the heart of worship yet it is easily set aside in the competing demands of life. It is at the juxtaposition of activity and silence. The soul is at its most active when we are still. 'Be still and know that I am God.' There are many techniques of prayer, one of which is to relax and quietly allow a thankfulness to emerge: to thank God for being alive in the present moment.

Silence is at the heart of prayer. True silence is different from the kind of contemplation that leads us into illusion. It is a silence that releases us into a knowledge of God's presence. 'Be still and know that I am God'. In true silence we bring others into the orbit as well. It leads to a kind of meditation where we pause to reflect before we do or say something unwise. Unfortunately much religion allows little time for this kind of silence. All too often it becomes loud, and even with an element of controversy to enliven matters. When we intercede for ourselves or for others it moves into prayer.

The other aspects of religion are less positive and can lead into politics of their own, which alas can become tainted with corruption. It is evident that religion has got to re-think its ends and means in order to play a positive role in the future. Life is finite which is why an appreciation of the present moment is so important, and its sharing with others. If only religion could better help us to achieve this.

Communication by silence may be achieved in retreats, where we get away from our daily lives in order to reflect. Silence is the most important element, since it allows us to reflect upon who and what we are. Few can bear it for long, which is why the retreat is also a group activity, but without the spoken word which can often be divisive. As the silence continues we may find we come to like those about whom we initially felt unsure. A retreat is not mainly about teaching. It is an adventure in getting to know one another that may lead to a loving appreciation. We do not learn to give retreats simply by attending courses. We also have to give of our life, which is the essential teacher. When I go on a retreat as conductor I relax and smile. I then enter into the kind of silence in which I can communicate individually and confidentially. I have often been told that I have said exactly what the retreatant needed to hear. This illustrates the power of the Holy Spirit because I certainly did not know the inner needs of those present. A retreat should be a time of enjoyment and uplift for all – provided they do not spoil it by note-taking, which may promote a feeling of work well done but inhibits the other valuable fruits of the retreat.

The spiritual way is one of conflict with the forces of this world, and we should accept this. 'Fight the good fight' is a hymn worth studying for it illustrates the positive approach to 'the fight of faith'.

Beauty and God

Beauty in the widest sense is of great importance for many people since it raises their aspirations above mundane everyday concerns towards the soul and towards God. Music and all the arts are essential for a mature civilisation. Music lifts us above ourselves. It enters our souls and brings us closer to the Divine. Jesus' first commandment was to love God and the arts help us to see the loveliness of the Creator. The classical composers such as Handel and Bach who inspire us, were succeeded by the romantics of the nineteenth century, and today we have the modern composers such as Stravinsky, John Taverner, and Samuel Barber all of whom I have come to appreciate.

Pictorial art is more immediate than music. One can be tone deaf to music, yet deeply moved by great painting or sculpture. Great as is the creative ability of great artists, yet paradoxically some of them have been very unpleasant people. Richard Wagner gave rise to the bigotry that led to Nazism, yet few would ignore his incomparable music. Gauguin was another example of this paradox. The ways of genius are indeed strange. And one can review the whole history of art and what it contributes to our life.

Then there is literature. In my view the Bible stands far above any other, in addition to its spiritual nature. In many respects the Old Testament goes further into human nature than the New Testament, mainly because it does not hesitate to record disgraceful episodes of human behaviour as well as the beatific. It is practical and honest. Especially there is the Book or Jeremiah and the Wisdom Literature, so that I could never become other than a Christian with strong Jewish roots.

The paradox in all this is the cruel treatment of Jesus. Oscar Wilde, in his 'Ballad of Reading Gaol' expresses this:-

'Each man kills the thing he loves ...' 'The coward does it with a kiss, the brave man with a sword'.

And yet there is Dame Julian of Norwich's reflection upon the tiny thing, like a hazel nut, that is yet everything and survives because God made it, God loves it, and God keeps it.

Finally there is the natural beauty that surrounds us. 'Consider the lilies of the field. They do not toil, neither do they spin. Yet Solomon in all his glory was not arrayed like one of these.' Each season brings forth its special beauty, even though winter can be cold and forbidding. God is the Creator, ruthless and terrible as well as glorious and life affirming. It is a part of the mystery of creation that evil is part of it and will not be removed by human endeavour. The way forward seems to be to devote care and tenderness to all creatures we meet, though this leaves a question as to what to do with the noxious elements of creation. Yet in Thomas Traherne's words, 'Till you can sing and rejoice and delight in God, as misers do in gold, and kings in sceptres, you never enjoy the world.'

Freedom – the Eternal Quest

We all desire freedom. We also misuse it. We desire wealth, power, love, and the liberty to do whatever we like. And having got all these, we become less and less satisfied. One reason for this is that freedom tends to direct us into ourselves and our personal goals. The one way of dealing with this paradox is by recognising it and living within it, seeking to direct our freedom toward the interests of the world around us. This of course is easier said than done. The more we try the more we fail. On a personal level we seek some reward. We like to be well regarded, but in this desire we forfeit our freedom for we are more than ever dependent upon what might be the whim of others.

The Buddhist preaches detachment, yet we know we are dependent upon a communal life. There are two impediments to freedom: impotence and licence. The impotent individual is in bondage to the more powerful, and until recently this was the position of women in western society. The licentious are prisoners of their own desires, a classical example being Don Juan.

While we are trapped in egoism we are not free. The Buddha said that all life is suffering, and Sophocles said, 'Call no man fortunate who is not dead, for the dead alone are free from pain.' All of this is very depressing. Yet one of the paradoxes is that to love others we must also love ourselves. It is fortunate that the Buddha also speaks of 'the middle way' which no extremist will find it possible to follow. In modern life we have the freedom of many social and communal benefits.

Political freedom implies democracy, where everyone is free to choose their own destiny, but within a legal framework. Dictatorship equals the opposite, yet are these poles quite what they seem? Winston Churchill commented that democracy was a terrible form of government – all the others were worse. The answer is to devote oneself to a life of communal involvement, which we can only do when we have ceased to regard ourselves as the centre of importance.

Religion helps us to do this, and when we have succeeded we have achieved freedom. Only when I accept that I can do very little in the time allotted to me can I take comfort and freedom in the present moment. 'Vanity, vanity, all is vanity' says the Preacher in the Book of Ecclesiastes, a part of the Wisdom Literature.

If a child were granted total freedom we all know that disaster would follow. For there to be true freedom there must also be responsibility. This is not always understood in our present age. Once we are subject to law – personal and civil – we are protected by barriers that enable us to feel safe and therefore free.

Freedom also demands that we respect the rights and the dignity of others. Other people will then respect us in like manner and so the structure of society is built up. This balance between freedom, responsibility, rights and dignity is especially important in families. Another essential element is humility. Without the willingness to accept that we are sometimes wrong we become parental family control freaks for all the reasons that we consider are most excellent.

Then there is power. Most oppressive regimes in history have been ultimately overthrown by the power of the people, save in the most advanced western societies where democracy has become virtually permanent.

Truth and Illusion

Truth can be viewed at many levels. It is most satisfactory when it can be proven as with present day scientific proof. But for us as individuals what matters is our belief system. This cannot be proved in the same way, save by experience. Hence when we try to bring science and religion together the results tend to be unsatisfactory, since people are apt to distort scientific principles to suit their own argument.

What is the truth about myself? What did I amount to as a young man, and what have I now become? What matters is my inner self. I may be outwardly handsome or ugly, but what is of concern is my inward integrity. Ideally we should all be aiming to 'Be perfect as your Father in Heaven is perfect'. This is of course beyond us save as a quest to be desired. And what is 'perfect' in the human sense? There is only so much truth that most of us can take, and he or she who tells less than perfect 'white lies' with a motive of pure love can hardly be less perfect that the one who kills with truthful but cruel unvarnished fact. And what about the person who steals from the rich to feed the poor, in various degrees, especially if you intended to repay the debt when you could?

If we look critically at ourselves we are likely to find many degrees of rectitude, or the lack of it, and many degrees of self-deception. Our lesson in spiritual development is to accept ourselves as we are, faults and all, and to let gratitude flow out to all around us without trying too hard to assess merit. 'Let us love one another, for love is of God.' And first of all we have to be able to love ourselves. Each of us has our own cast of personality: humour, or the lack of it; introvert or extravert; fanatical or broad in outlook; happy or solemn. These characteristics apply to ordinary folk and celebrities alike – even dictators, though they in particular tend to have an essentially negative aspect that leads to the atrocities they allow.

Perhaps the most important gift is a balanced sense of humour that enables us to see ourselves and others in perspective. If we knew the truth about ourselves this would set us free. And as we grow older our self-knowledge develops. Perhaps our end should be to have well-rounded genuine personalities rather than to concentrate on being good, whatever this may mean. The Sermon on the Mount is hard to encompass all at once, but if inculcated into us when young, it ensures that we will grow into an attitude of love towards our fellow beings. Truth on a moral level is universal. It exists within all religions, which practise it daily, and not only upon special occasions. And so much of public secular life today is full of illusions – none more so than within the cult of the celebrity in present-day media.

Our attitude is the way in which we confront our daily lives. When young we are proscribed by what we can achieve. As we grow our horizons widen. 'Spare the rod and spoil the child' is unpopular today but it does have its merits to a degree, since it guards against the cult of the individual, whereby 'I can have everything I want, and I am not responsible for anybody else' and became the way of the 1980s.

Integrity of character forms as we grow in experience. The Seven Deadly Sins continue to define the level of integrity we possess, the deadliest arguably being Pride, Avarice and Lust.

As I have grown older I have experienced a measure of clinical depression that has defined what I am to a degree. I have also had the leisure to contemplate life in the next world, which I do not perceive as beatifically as some religious people view it. I see it as a further period of development in which the unfinished business of this life will have to be concluded; in which the 'unsaved' will interact uneasily with the 'saved' so that there will eventually be one united host. This is the meaning of heaven, when all is united. It is indeed a mystery and it will take time, possibly in another dimension. The religions of the East allow reincarnation within which this might happen. The West is resolutely opposed to the idea.

But much of this is conjecture. In the words of John Keats 'Beauty is truth, and truth beauty' and that is all we need to know on earth.

The Quest for Happiness

This book is about happiness yet it has shown how hard it can be to achieve. The Buddha observed that human desire is the cause of much unhappiness, yet without it nothing could be achieved. Happiness is a state of mind in which one's present circumstances are accepted. Adversity can detract from one's happiness, and a sense of humour can be an essential companion. Happiness does not depend upon having anything at all but on being content with what one has got. My own happiness was constrained by my upbringing and circumstances, and by psychic sensitivity which can itself be painful and has set me apart from many other people. Yet it was these constraints that made me what I am.

I have in these pages been harsh in what I have said of conventional religion. Yet far worse in my view is the current style of dominant rationalism that cannot permit anything to be contemplated that cannot directly be proved by science. I have no doubt that there is much to life that cannot be proved by pure reason. A deeper power of the soul is necessary before we can know the reality of the self. When we know this ultimate truth a higher degree of happiness will become ours. As Julian of Norwich wrote, 'Sin is behovable, but all shall be well, and all shall be well, and all manner of thing shall be well.'

I myself am something of a puzzle: an ethnic Jew, a Christian priest and a spiritual universalist. Despite losing cousins in the Holocaust I cannot support an Israeli state that dispossesses its Palestinian neighbours. If one is chosen by God your whole life is sacrifice, and that is its reward and happiness. I am one of the few humans who have seen the other side of death, and I know what a great work is the ministry of deliverance and bringing light into what was darkness.

I believe the Buddha to be the great World Teacher. Jesus Christ is the great World Exemplar. I like Hinduism and Buddhism for their indifference to seeking converts. What I dislike about Christianity and Islam is their constant seeking for converts, which alas comes across not so much as a spread of enlightenment as the means of self-aggrandisement among the purveyors. The Jews have erred in the other direction – that of exclusivity. I consider the hope of world religion lies in mystical liberalism, in which the enlightened mind is illuminated by a love which rises above reason – the essence of God Himself. Without it I see destruction ahead. With it we may begin to see heaven on earth.

10. Summaries of Other Publications

Living Alone – The Inward Journey to Fellowship

In present times much of society seems dedicated to the cult of the family, and to be generally accepted that one has to be a 'team player'. This book however is dedicated to those many people who for one reason or another have no family or do not belong to any team. Living alone, Martin Israel says, is a very individual experience which each one pursues in their own way, as he has done. He explores the inner life of a person, and the path to an awareness that, in becoming a fully adjusted person, can ultimately lead to a knowledge of God.

SPCK – 1982

The Spirit of Counsel - Perspectives in the Counselling Process

Counselling is of increasing importance in the modern world of frantic and stressful activity when no one seems to have time to offer a listening ear. The counsellor needs a comprehensive vision of life in which the various discordant aspects of existence can be seen in a wider context. This book indicates how silent trust and openness to wisdom, especially the wisdom of God, can take counsellor closer to client, bringing a superior level of understanding that leads from fear and perplexity into truth.

Hodder & Stoughton – 1983

The Discipline of Love – The Ten Commandments for Today

The Ten Commandments were imparted to Moses upon Mount Sinai, and have formed the basis of morality throughout the Judeo-Christian tradition. Later they were to be distilled into the principles of love 'upon which hangs all the law and the prophets'. In the present age each generation seems to feel it necessary to revisit its morals, which are in effect merely 'the customs of the people'. In reminding us that human love requires discipline, Dr Israel reviews the ten principles upon which ethics have been based over the centuries, and which arguably have stood the test of time if sensibly and intelligently applied.

SPCK – 1985

Coming in Glory – Christ's Presence in the World Today

The theme of this book is the coming of Christ, the Word of God, in the universe. He was in the very beginning. He is present in the souls of all rational creatures, finding his summation in the person of Jesus of Nazareth. He is with us when we are truly human, and when we are ready we will be changed and will see him as he really is. After chapters covering freedom, detachment, the trials of life, death and judgement, Martin Israel depicts the final triumphal resurrection when creatures shall no longer hurt or destroy and in which the land shall be filled with the glory of God as the waters cover the sea.

Darton Longman & Todd – 1986

Gethsemane – the Transfiguring Love

Chosen as the Archbishop of Canterbury's Lent Book for that year, there is a foreword by Archbishop Robert Runcie who suggests that Martin Israel here offers a wealth of understanding and wisdom in the theology of redemption, including an understanding of pain. Suffering in this life is necessary but if we can persevere to the end, there is the Peace of God which surpasses all mankind's understanding.

Collins – 1987

The Pearl of Great Price – A Journey to the Kingdom

The Pearl of Great Price is the symbol of the kingdom of heaven, to obtain which, a merchant sold all that he had, in order to buy. It can come to us as a vision when we least expect it, hinting at future happiness and fulfilment. Then it disappears leaving us with a haunting memory. It cannot simply be seized. We have to wait until a time in our life when we can use it properly, often after a previous sacrifice or travail of some kind. Martin Israel offers us the outline of a journey, at the end of which we may hope to achieve the Assumption of this Pearl.

SPCK – 1988

Creation – the Consummation of the World

The author turns to the subject of creation and creativity. He analyses recent research by anthropologists and physicists in the light of his own understanding of the Bible, suggesting that to realise our full potential we have to 'create in the shadow of God'. To be a Christian does not mean being religious in a particular way, but to be a full, mature human being. Then our spiritual body is well formed within us and blessings flow from us to the world, which is thereby transfigured.

Fount Paperbacks – 1989

The Dark Face of Reality – A Study of Emergent Awareness

In life we experience two kinds of darkness: the kind that afflicts us through personal misfortune, and also the overall power of evil in the world that assails us through wars and civil disorder or atrocity. Dr Israel invites us to examine not only the nature of evil but also its ultimate healing. He offers a sight of the ultimate reality, the love of God, and a hope so precious that all past suffering seems logical and containable.

Fount Paperbacks – 1989

The Quest for Wholeness

A medical doctor by profession, Martin Israel opens this book with a description of how he first experienced spiritual healing by the laying on of hands, which alleviated his severe allergy in the summer of 1962. Despite his training in scientific medicine, this event was to prove crucial in the establishment of a healing ministry that he was soon to undertake. Giving case histories anonymously, the author emphasises some of the strengths and pitfalls of spiritual healing. It is God, through the Holy Spirit who heals, not the healer. Some people have healing gifts; others do not. It is a vocation to be recognised rather than to be desired. A temptation is the wish for power or influence as a healer which must be resisted. Spiritual healing is primarily about healing the soul. Physical wholeness may or may not be a by-product. Paradoxically the ultimate healing is that brought by death itself, which opens into victory.

Darton, Longman & Todd – 1989

A Light on the Path – Exploring Integrity through the Psalms

The reader is invited to share in what Dr Israel describes as 'this treasury of human spiritual experience'. The psalms, the religious poetry of Israel, have been used in private prayer and in public worship down the ages, having relevance today as they had in former centuries. They offer many proverbial phrases, affording us a light upon the sometimes dark places of our lives, and inspiring us to 'take the wings of the morning' and rise above our tribulations.

Darton, Longman & Todd – 1990

Night Thoughts

This book is primarily intended for those whose lives are sufficiently ordered for them to set aside a little time each day, preferably at night, to meditate or reflect upon truths that transcend the tribulations of daily life. Containing eight meditations in all, they invite us to reflect upon the course of our lives and to examine the truths that underlie our actions and attitudes. Each one contains a text, a brief chapter, and a short prayer. And, as if for those of us for whom such self-discipline seems out of reach, there is the quotation from Dame Julian of Norwich: 'He said not "Thou shall not be tempested, thou shall not be travailed, thou shall not be afflicted"; but he said "Thou shall not be overcome"'.

SPCK – 1990

Life Eternal

Dedicated to his old friend Leslie Price who is learned in the field of parapsychology, data is marshalled to support the view that brain and mind, body and soul, are in fact two separate categories, marvellously linked while we are alive. Whilst respecting the necessary agnosticism of the scientist, Martin Israel explores the powerful evidence for survival after death. This is suggested by those who have survived Near-Death Experiences, and by the work of mediums and by memories of past lives that some people profess. He seeks to comfort the bereaved and to offer the hope contained in the Nicene Creed of 'the Resurrection of the Dead and the Life of the World to come.'

SPCK – 1992

Dark Victory - Through Depression to Hope

We are all subject to changing moods. Positive moods can energise us. Negative moods can debilitate us, depriving us of hope and making us want to withdraw from everything and from everyone. All of these moods have their value, however, and have something to offer the sensitive person. It is said that 'the man is greater than the mood' – and the woman likewise. Out of our suffering can come our greatest joy, like the mother who rejoices after the pangs of childbirth.

Mowbray – 1995

Angels - Messengers of Grace

This book looks at angels, traditionally the messengers of God and recognised by all the Abrahamic faiths. It examines their influence upon ordinary people, which to this day is significant. *(In 2011 a survey in USA reported that 77% of Americans believed in angels, and over half of those surveyed claimed that they had been helped by a guardian angel at some time in life).* Supported by Dr Israel's several friends who provided accounts of angelic appearances, the text examines angels in the Old and New Testaments of the Bible, the experience and properties of angels both in darkness and in light, and what angels may have to teach us. There are extensive references in an appendix, and suggestions for further reading.

SPCK – 1995

Doubt - The Way of Growth

Religious people are often told they should have faith, and when it deserts them they feel inadequate. Yet personal experience shows that doubt is a part of living, especially in the modern age where truths that have been asserted through the ages are constantly being challenged. Facing our doubts in the right way and learning to grow through them is part of our journey from the dark places of our lives towards the integrity that comes with embracing 'the sacrament of the present moment'. We then reach a state that Dr Israel calls true equanimity, which leads us to be open to receive love and to pass it to others – the true way to salvation for each one of us.

Mowbray – 1997

Exorcism - The Removal of Evil Influences

Dr Martin Israel approaches this much misunderstood subject in an unemotional and professional manner from the viewpoint of the experienced practitioner. He warns that only those who have experience of special psychic gifts or sensitivity should become involved in such matters, and that most of us should develop our religious faith in more fruitful ways. But there are nonetheless instances where deliverance is necessary, both to free those who are being assailed by psychic forces, and also to allow those influences, if such they be, themselves to pass on to their proper destiny. Exorcism is the ejection of an undesirable psychic entity from a person or a place where they are causing mischief. The ministry of deliverance – a more wholesome approach – is the handing over of the mischievous entity to God's care. In an age of scientific materialism where all such matters tend to be regarded as solely within the field of the psychiatrist, this book is a valuable primer.

SPCK – 1997

The Devout Life

This book was written and published a few years after Martin Israel had retired. Compiled jointly with the Revd Neil Broadbent, founder of Sozein, a Churches Ministry of Healing Trust in Derbyshire, it acknowledges help given by the Revd Robert Llewellyn, Chaplain of the Cell of Dame Julian of Norwich, and by Dr Peta Dunston of Cambridge Divinity School Library. It is based upon the spiritual genius of William Law, author of *'A Serious Call to a Devout and Holy Life'*, a best seller in 1726. Opening with a robust but edited quotation from Philip Larkin, 'They muck you up, your mum and dad; they may not mean to, but they do!', there follows an analysis of divine love as depicted by William Law in all its complexities and forms, with extensive end notes and references. It finishes with the message of Jesus Christ, the Light of the World: 'Behold, I stand at the door and knock. If any man hear my voice and open the door, I will come in to him and will sup with him.'

Continuum - 2001

London Reflections – A Parish Priest Writes to his Parishioners in South Kensington
and
Discipleship Today – Addresses to a Congregation in London

These two booklets record a selection of Martin Israel's short written addresses in his monthly parish magazines and also transcriptions of some of his tape-recorded sermons which were always delivered inspirationally and without written notes.

CFPSS – 2001 and 2002 respectively

11. The Spiritual Wisdom of Martin Israel

Martin wrote over twenty books, on a wide variety of subjects: evil, counselling, healing, the spiritual journey, wholeness, depression, doubt, the second coming, angels, exorcism, happiness – to mention only a few. What he did not do was to write a guide to the spiritual life, or a manual for spiritual directors, as others have done. His teaching about the spiritual life has to be carefully gleaned from his many books and the tapes of his many lectures. This chapter attempts to summarise briefly some of the central themes of his teaching. It hardly needs to be emphasised that a chapter as short as this can do no more than skate over the surface of his work – and perhaps inspire the readers to experience the richness of Martin's writing for him or herself.

Before we can proceed further, we need to confront two of the demons which so beset him and two puzzling aspects of his life and writing. As John Wyborn makes clear in his biography of Martin, he grew up in an affluent home in Johannesburg, South Africa. His father was a successful and respected doctor. As a child he lacked nothing in terms of his physical care and he was sent to private schools. Yet, hard though it is to believe, Martin was subjected to sexual abuse by his father. The emotional trauma caused by this, resulted, not surprisingly, in a lack of self-confidence and self-worth that plagued him for the rest of his life and for which he seemed to find no real healing. In writing about the importance of doubt in our lives and especially in the making of moral decisions, he states that we should have a non-judgemental attitude to all forms of sexual behaviour, except the sexual abuse of children. In writing about Christ's command to take up your cross and follow me, he also says that we do not have to seek a cross to bear in our lives. The cross we have to bear may be some wound that prevents us fulfilling ourselves in this world.

Those words must surely have been written from the depths of his own heart and the awfulness of his own experience. Nevertheless, there are some who find Martin's claim to sexual abuse impossible to believe and search for some explanation amidst the complexities of child psychology. Understandable as this may be, we have to recognise that Martin was a man of probity who was unlikely to make allegations so damaging to the character and reputation of his own father unless there was at least some grounding in truth. We do not and cannot know what took place. Martin attributed his lack of self-worth to this experience. That, we should understand and respect.

As his name implies, Martin was born a Jew and grew up in a Jewish family. He was very conscious of the troubled history of the Jewish people and of his kinship with members of his family who lived in Jewish communities in Europe. In the course of the Second World War many of these were murdered in the Holocaust. This gave Martin not just an acute awareness of the reality of human evil, but an even deeper awareness of the mystery of the existence of evil at all. In his book *Angels*, Martin confronts this issue head on. He affirms with great clarity – as Isaiah did centuries before – that 'it cannot be denied that God is the ultimate cause of evil'. He continues, 'Evil appears to be an integral part of the process of creation. Mystics see God as beyond good and evil as these are categories limited to human understanding'. Elsewhere he writes, 'The problem of evil and a God of love cannot be solved at an intellectual level'. Martin concludes that when confronting suffering and evil, we enter a cloud of unknowing and our only guide is our faith. For Martin, this faith was, of course, his strong belief in the resurrection of Christ as symbolising God's ultimate triumph over evil and all the brokenness of creation. But this was not an act of faith which came easily to him and the obscene monstrosity of evil was a demon which haunted him to the end of his life.

We should now reflect on the two puzzling aspects of Martin's life and work insofar as they relate to his teaching and his beliefs.

Between 1976 and 2001, Martin wrote over twenty books on various aspects of the spiritual life. For these he had in those years a sizeable and faithful readership. Implicit in all that he wrote, was his own personal and very orthodox understanding of the faith of the Church as expressed in the traditional creeds. It seems that by the mid 1960s, he had come through to what many still accepted at the time – a scholarly understanding of the Christian faith much in the tradition of Archbishops Michael Ramsay and Donald Coggan and an understanding of the authority of the Bible much in sympathy with

New Testament scholars like Professor C. H. Dodd and Professor William Barclay. His faithfulness to orthodoxy emerges everywhere throughout his writing and his lectures. He constantly emphasises the centrality of the doctrine of the Trinity: that the godhead of the Father, of the Son and of the Holy Spirit is all one, the glory equal, the majesty co-eternal. He affirms the doctrine of the incarnation, that our Lord Jesus Christ, the Son of God, is both God and Man. He constantly emphasises the doctrine of the atonement whereby Christ on the Cross made a full, perfect and sufficient sacrifice, oblation and satisfaction for the sins of the whole world. The extent to which his mind was steeped in a traditionalist interpretation of the Bible emerges in his comments on all the many biblical passages which he uses to illustrate his teaching. No one could have accused Martin of being subversively radical in his personal beliefs. The puzzling aspect of this is that the years during which he was writing were years of radical criticism and controversy across the whole field of Christian theology and biblical studies. To mention only a few of the more responsible scholars who were influential during this time: in 1977 Professor John Hick of the University of Birmingham, published *The Myth of God Incarnate* to be followed a few years later by *The Metaphor of God Incarnate*. In these books he claims that Jesus never taught what was to become the Church's teaching about him and that the whole concept of a theology of sin and redemption relates to a vanished world.

In 1984, the Revd Don Cupitt, Fellow of Emmanuel College, Cambridge, presented on peak time TV, his series of programmes on *The Sea of Faith,* outlining for millions of viewers some of the many reasons for the decline in Christian belief and in the authority of the Bible throughout the western world. In a later book, *After God,* published in 1997, Don Cupitt declared that all religions, including Christianity, are products of the human imagination. All that remains of Christianity is the vision of Christ as an exemplar of compassionate love.

Throughout the 1980s and 1990s the Jesus Seminar was at work in the U.S.A. This was a group of some 150 New Testament scholars who met regularly to vote, line by line, on the authenticity or otherwise of the four gospels. They concluded that the Jesus of the gospels is an imaginative theological construct into which have been woven traces of the sage of Nazareth. It was their view that 82% of the words ascribed to Jesus in the gospels are not his. The Christian myth should be seen as a human creation not as revealed truth.

In his book, *For Christ's Sake,* published in 1993, Tom Harpur, a former Professor of New Testament in the University of Toronto declared that Jesus is a mythical figure, though his story is myth of the highest order; that the doctrines of the Trinity and Incarnation are now largely meaningless as is the substitutionary theology of the atonement. The whole blood sacrifice myth is from the most primitive religious thinking of the ancient world.

Amongst the many feminist theologians who were prominent at this time was Professor Daphne Hampson of the University of St Andrews who in her book *After Christianity* published in 1996, described Christianity as an outdated and discredited male patriarchal myth. All that remains is the respect we should have for the validity of individual religious experience.

These books which have been mentioned are only a few among a very large literature. Their authors are not fanatical atheists out to discredit religion in all its forms. They are responsible scholars holding academic appointments and either believers in, or sympathetic to, the Christian faith. The puzzle is that no breath of all this prolonged and serious controversy and criticism appears in Martin's writing. We have to ask, 'How can this be?' He was far too intelligent and widely read to be unaware of its existence. There are at least two possible lines of speculation.

Martin grew up as a Jew and was educated in the Liberal Jewish tradition. Over the years he gradually moved away from this and eventually converted to Christianity. Understandably enough, Judaism gives conversion to Christianity strong spiritual and social discouragement. For a man of Martin's spiritual and mystical sensitivity, this cannot have been an easy process. As the years passed and as he became successfully established in the medical profession, he found time for the prayer, thought and study involved in developing his own understanding of the Christian faith, an understanding which was remarkably orthodox and based on the creeds. Perhaps as a convert he may have felt that it was not his place to question orthodox beliefs but rather to accept a faith affirmed by the Church for centuries and sanctified by the devotion of many millions of the faithful. Perhaps Martin came to find that traditional orthodoxy provided him with the grounding which he needed for his life and ministry. Perhaps he also realised that involvement in the theological controversies of the time might, quite simply, destroy him; that he would end up like one of Milton's fallen angels 'in wandering mazes lost'. Reginald Somerset Ward was one of the leading spiritual directors of the Church of England in the years between the 1930s and the 1960s. In one of his books he wrote, 'Many Christian souls start out on their spiritual journey with much spiritual baggage but they end up with the creed, trust, love and humility and find that these will carry them to the gates of Jerusalem'. Perhaps it was something like that Martin discovered for himself.

The second line of speculation relates to Martin's training for the ministry – or rather, the lack of it. He was ordained in 1974 by the then Bishop of London, Gerald Ellison. For many years it had been the custom for bishops to ordain certain public school headmasters, academics and schoolmasters without formal ministerial training. It was assumed that as able men they could follow a course of reading for themselves. Before the growth of theological colleges in the 19th century this had been the norm. It is not recorded that Martin had any formal university based training in theology.

It may be that Martin felt that should he wish to become involved in medical controversy, he would be fully entitled to do so on the grounds of his qualifications, status and experience. By contrast he may have felt that he was not entitled to become involved in theological and biblical controversy because of his lack of academic credentials. This is not to imply that Martin's orthodoxy was in any sense a mindless acceptance of 'the teachings of the Church'. As will be made clear later, he stressed the importance of each person giving the words of the creeds his or her own personal meaning and understanding.

Confronting the second puzzle relates to our need to try to understand Martin as a person. He was one of the post war generation of young men who were conscripted for two years National Service, in his case in the Army. Unlike those drafted in for service in the infantry, the artillery or tanks, he was not required to undergo the very arduous and physically demanding three months course of basic training. As a qualified doctor, Martin entered the Army as a Captain in the Royal Army Medical Corps. He would have had to attend what was called the 'Professionally Qualified Officer Course' at the Royal Military Academy, Sandhurst. This was a four-week initiation course for clergy, doctors, nurses, physiotherapists and others joining the Army from professional work or training. The British Army is a world of its own with its own traditions, loyalties, procedures and disciplines. Martin, straight from medical school and hospital training would need initiation into this if he was not to be totally bewildered. As a medical officer he would have been welcomed by the men of his regiment with genuine respect and with cheerful and no less genuine respect in the officers' mess where he lived. As his time of service was in the 'cold war' and so the Army was not everywhere on active service, his medical duties would have been fairly minimal, and would have given him ample time for his own studies. It could well be that as time went on, and with his lack of social ease, he found the alcoholic joviality of the officers mess increasingly difficult to live with. It could also very well be that he came to have a profound horror of the whole military context. The Army exists to defend the realm by killing the enemy. This is a ruthless, brutal and bloody business however much it may be glamorised by brass bands and splendid uniforms. Perhaps a man of his personal, moral, psychic and spiritual sensitivity found the whole experience purgatorial – for in all his writing he scarcely mentions it. This is strange, as most men who completed National Service found the experience unforgettable, for better or for worse. Martin seems to have wanted only to remove every trace of it from his memory.

These reflections make clear to us that Martin's life was not one of peace and tranquillity, lived out in the calm of the cloister and the library. Quite the opposite. All his teaching about the spiritual life is grounded in the realities of human experience and on this subject he was no starry-eyed optimist. In his book, *Coming in Glory,* he speaks of 'the raging agony of life'. Human life, he writes, 'despite periods of glitter is essentially dark'. Elsewhere he writes that 'the spiritual journey starts when we awake from the pointlessness of much daily life'. In his book, *Dark Victory*, he admits that for him, *Ecclesiastes* is the most refreshing book in the Bible for it is a chronicle of pessimism about the world and human life and the vanity of all earthly striving. He quotes with approval the words of William Blake:-

Joy and Woe are woven fine,
A clothing for the soul divine.

It is in the context of a compassionate understanding of the life of this complex man that we can now attempt a brief study of the central aspects of his teaching. It cannot be emphasised strongly enough that all his teaching about spirituality was influenced not so much by academic study as by the realities of his own inner, personal spiritual and psychic experience.

The Inner Life

Martin constantly stresses the absolute importance of the inner life. We are, he emphasises, spiritual beings and the quality of our inner spiritual life affects every aspect of our existence, for better or for worse, both here and hereafter. Spiritual growth is the central purpose of our life. The spiritual experience of the centuries makes clear that there are certain practices which enhance this.

Private Prayer

Some regular and faithful private prayer comes first, though Martin wisely specifies no one particular method. He comments that there are as many ways of effective prayer as there are people who pray.

Contemplation and Meditation

These have their place of special importance so long as much time is given to the practice of silence. It is in silence that God the Holy Spirit may best communicate with us. On this subject he remarks that the principal use of religion is the practice of prayer and silence.

Intercession

Intercession will have its important place in private prayer as it is the means whereby what he calls 'rapt prayer' can bring the power of the Holy Spirit to the needs of people and events. 'Rapt prayer' is not the same as the rattling off of lists of names. While recognising the place of confession, Martin sees little value in prolonged and detailed outpourings of sin and guilt. Like Baron von Hügel he sees no value in starting each day with a spiritual flea hunt. Sin became the obsession of the Church; it was never so with Christ. By contrast, time should be given to detailed thanksgiving. In this Martin affirms the statements of the 14th century mystic, Meister Eckhart, 'If you have only one prayer, let it be a prayer of gratitude' and the 18th century spiritual writer William Law, 'could you work miracles, you could not do more than live in the spirit of thankfulness for it transforms all that it touches'.

Together with private prayer, Martin affirms the value and importance of regular participation in the liturgical and sacramental life of the Church. But he does not seem to see this as a strict obligation. He points out that there is no account in the New Testament of Jesus interrogating anyone about their religious observance. He was concerned with their inner life and state of mind.

Martin sees private prayer and faithful participation in the Eucharistic worship of the Church as the means whereby we may develop our understanding of what De Caussade describes as the sacrament of the present moment. By this, our spiritual awareness extends to every aspect of our life, including the demands and responsibilities of our daily work and living. Martin insists, very strongly, that our spiritual life is not just limited to our private devotions, however important they may be. He states with great clarity that 'our daily work is part of our spiritual life and our attention should be fully on it'.

It is by spiritual disciplines such as these, Martin affirms, that we may attune ourselves to the being of God and to the energies of the Holy

Spirit at work within us. This enables our gradual inner transformation whereby we come to realise our oneness with God and whereby, by slow degrees, the gifts of the Spirit may grow within us. As he says, 'this is our way to wholeness and to a sense of meaning and purpose in life. When we are put to the test it is the inner life alone that can sustain us'.

God

Despite his faithfulness to the words of the creed, Martin insists that we have to ask ourselves: What do these words mean and what do they mean to me? It is clear that when Martin speaks of God he is not talking about the angry old man with a beard in the sky of popular caricature. I am grateful to the Revd Neil Broadbent for pointing out that Martin's definition of God is to be found on p.52 of his book *Life Eternal*, 'A presence of spiritual aspiration beyond myself by which my life is guided to the light'. Elsewhere he writes, 'We cannot give a name to the ultimate source of being from whom all creation comes. God transcends all categories and is the reality behind every form. We know him through his outflowing energies, love, light and wisdom.'

In his book on *Doubt*, Martin writes, 'The point about God is that nothing positive can be said about him until we know that nothing negative can be said about him. We come to know God primarily by being silent. We cannot know God by the intellect at all. The best we can do is to be silent before him. 'By love he may be gotten and holden, by thought never.' As we might expect, Martin speaks of God not in the language of academic theology but in the language of mysticism. That was for him, his way to truth.

The Person of Christ

Central to Martin's faith and to every aspect of his teaching is the person of Christ; Christ, Son of God and second person of the Trinity, Christ the Saviour who by his atoning death on the cross takes away the sin of the world, the inner Christ active in the life of every Christian, the cosmic Christ active through all the divine energies that sustain all creation, Christ the teacher, Christ who is our vision of God: 'He that hath seen me hath seen the Father'. To do justice to the place of Christ in Martin's thought would require not just another chapter but another book. The origin of Martin's devotion to the person of Christ dates back to his childhood in Johannesburg. One of the African servants in his home left, lying about, a missionary tract about the life and ministry of Jesus. It was reading this that began his long progress from a conventional Jewish faith to his passionately dedicated Christian faith.

The Life after Death

Martin was very clear that death is not the end and that a belief in the life after death is built into our human consciousness. His beliefs on this subject may be briefly summarised: We continue to live after the experience we call death since the energies of God are energies of love and it is this love that ensures our future in this world and the next. Our life is the product of divine love and our immortality is the manifestation of that caring.

Martin is emphatic that the phenomenon called this world is only the surface of reality. Ours is not a world of finality. Beyond this is the realm of ultimate reality whose nature is divine. There we live in the spiritual body, the quality of which will be determined by our thoughts, words and actions in this life. If we have no spiritual reserves there will be little to accompany us into the life beyond death. As we have sown love in our personal relationships in this life, so will we be greeted with love in the hereafter. He does not attempt to go into the kind of detail about the hereafter that we find, e.g. in Swedenborg's massive work, *Heaven and Hell.*

He does see each one of us as a work in progress, whose purpose is spiritual growth either by continuing on higher planes of existence in the cosmos or by reincarnation into the life of this world. This would be to complete some task we felt to be important or to help in some way to diminish human suffering. Death is not a once and for all event, he remarks. Martin confirms that his own fear of death was totally removed by a near-death experience, as it has been for countless thousands of others.

Perhaps rather surprisingly, given his own psychic and spiritual sensitivities he counsels great caution when considering the claims of mediums to have contact with the dead. He accepts that there are a few gifted mediums whose integrity can be trusted but that this whole field has been so discredited by fraud that there be no grounds for any kind of easy credulity.

Martin's position seems close to that of St Paul whose words have been read at so many funerals, 'Now this I say, brethren, that flesh and blood cannot inherit the kingdom of God; neither doth corruption inherit incorruption. Behold, I shew you a mystery; We shall not all sleep but we shall all be changed'. And what we shall be changed into, by the power of the Holy Spirit, Martin suggests, is a transfiguration more magnificent than anything we can even begin to imagine.

The Shadow Side

Martin insists, firmly and in strong language, that we have a shadow side – a divided consciousness – and that we should not try to delude ourselves that we do not. As in the course of our spiritual life the grace of the Holy Spirit works within us so we may grow in the gifts of the Spirit, faith, hope, love, patience, goodness and wisdom. We may also grow in our sense of humour. As Martin remarks, wherever a sense of humour is present and alive, the Holy Spirit is never far away. But we have another side altogether to our inner life.

As he writes in *Coming in Glory*, 'the presence of Christ within may lead us to self-discovery and into our private cesspit of corruption. As Christ mixed with the common people in their thoughtless degradation so we may have to come to terms with the gamut of disturbance within our own personality'. He continues, 'Our demons are within us, anger, hatred, jealousy, lust, bitterness, resentment and above all, fear. These demons of darkness can produce destructive and negative thoughts, especially in times of stress and sickness. We cannot escape the reality of ourselves. We all have some inner defect to confront and perhaps even to affirm'.

He also points out that we share our divided consciousness with the divided consciousness of the whole of humanity, a reality amply demonstrated by all human history. But Martin reminds us that the regeneration of our personality is one of the important aspects of our spiritual life and our guard against the evil effects of our shadow side is the presence of the Holy Spirit constantly at work within us.

The Angels

On perhaps a more cheerful note, Martin affirms his belief in the existence and ministry of angels. In his book on the subject he writes, 'Within the cosmos and so within the life of this world, this plane of existence, there exists an order of beings spiritual in nature who are able to convey divine energies to all that live. Normally invisible to us, they can on occasions appear as humans. They can be idioplastic – i.e. capable of a variety of appearances'. Angels are referred to in the writings of all world faiths as well as the Old and New Testaments.

His own belief in the angels is grounded in his personal spiritual expepience and he recognises the existence of a large literature on the subject of angelic encounters. The validity of an encounter may be proved by the subsequent quality of life of the person concerned. It is probable that the being of light referred to by so many when describing their near-death experience is one of the angelic beings who help souls through the psycho-spiritual realm between this world and the next.

But however positive he may be on this subject, he emphasises that doubt, reason and a critical awareness still have to be retained. We have to be on our guard against fantasy and self-delusion. As with so many issues on which he writes, Martin the scientist and the doctor is never far away.

The Ministry of Healing

Martin affirms that the source of all healing is the energy of God at work through surgery, physical medicine, the laying on of hands or the prayer of the intercessor. He also recognises that within the churches the 'ministry of healing' has become, in recent years, much more generally accepted. He points out that there are requirements for those who wish to be active in this ministry: a clear sense of calling, a deep openness to God and a loving concern for our fellow humans. In this ministry we are alongside the patient, not distant or superior to him or her. There is no place for egotism or vanity, only a realisation, in humility, that the healer is only a channel for the healing power of the Holy Spirit.

Martin recognises a variety of methods in this ministry; the laying on of hands, anointing, counselling, confession and absolution when the barrier to healing may be guilt or shame, the administration of the Eucharist. But at the heart of it all is what he calls 'assiduous prayer in silence and deep recollection'. He warns that requests for the ministry of healing all too often relate to the healing of some symptom rather than the whole person. What may be required is the raising of a person's consciousness by the work of the Holy Spirit resulting in a gradual transfiguration of that person's whole understanding of life. This may involve faithful treatment over many weeks.

Martin also recognises that there are persons with no religious affiliation who possess an innate gift of healing; a gift which they discovered and are entirely unable to explain. Their ministry, he says, should be accepted if it is affirmed by positive results. Healing is a ministry with many dimensions. In his book, *Dark Victory,* Martin discusses the many problems created by medical conditions such as severe birth deformities, crippling incurable diseases and prolonged total dementia. He asks the very searching question: 'Is life always great?' In a recent book, Professor Paul Badham presents, *A Christian Case for Assisted Dying*. I suspect that Martin would have been one of his strong supporters.

The Ministry of Deliverance

Martin was a man of psychic sensitivity so was able to speak of exorcism and deliverance with a greater degree of confidence than those of us whose psychic sensitivity is less evident. Nevertheless, he speaks of this whole subject with caution. He emphasises that psychic gifts are gifts, and should not be sought. All world religions view such gifts with extreme reticence. On matters psychic there is a large and uncertain borderland between reality, mental illness, fantasy and fraud.

As well as men of great evil, such as Adolf Hitler, it is Martin's belief that there are evil energies and entities alive everywhere within the cosmos – perhaps the 'principalities and powers' referred to by St Paul. There are also entities he describes as 'the unquiet dead', discarnate beings who, for various reasons, have been unable or unwilling to move on after death into the next life.

The ministry of deliverance involves the ejection of an undesirable entity from a person or a place. Martin emphasises most strongly that not all clergy are called to this ministry; only a very few with a strong sense of calling and with the necessary gift of psychic discernment. This gift will enable the minister to distinguish between reality and illusion. A rational explanation should always be expected. Only when this has been fully ruled out should any attempt be made at a ministry of deliverance, e.g. by prayer, blessing, the laying on of hands or the celebration of the Eucharist.

Martin speculates that occasionally the unquiet dead may include the soul of an aborted foetus. On this issue it is worth noting that the Stillbirth and Neonatal Death Society has, in recent years, been concerned to ensure that an aborted foetus is not just disposed of as clinical waste but commended to God in a way appropriate to the wishes of the parents or parent. The whole subject is, of course, highly contentious. Perhaps, rather wisely, Martin seems not to have elaborated further upon it.

The Future

Martin could not have been described as what used to be called a 'sound churchman'. He did not concern himself with issues like liturgical renewal or the revision of diocesan boundaries. Had he been elected to the General Synod it seems unlikely that he would have made impassioned speeches about gays, lesbians and women bishops. He sat loose to the concept of ecclesiastical authority and would have been in sympathy with Lady Violet Bonham Carter's remark about the absurdity of 'a group of elderly Italian bachelors' presuming to lecture British women about their sex lives.

Martin emphasises that authority in the spiritual life is your own, influenced by prayer, worship, the intelligent study of scripture, awareness of the tradition of the Church, thought, reading and the exercise of critical reason. But a central place has to be given to reflection on your own experience of life. He would have agreed with Bultmann's statement, 'You should do theology out of your own story'. If your spiritual life is to have any meaning for you, it will be the product of your own mind and heart, not a hand-me-down from some guru or committee.

Relaxed as he was about the future of the institutional church, he was deeply concerned about the future of religious faith. In his book, *Coming in Glory,* he writes, 'In modern times there have been episodes of religious revival and nearly all of these have followed an arid period of intellectual enlightenment or a phase of moral permissiveness. This sequence testifies to the spiritually barren world of intellectual speculation, scientific research, social experimentation and sensual stimulation in the absence of a living faith. These modes of human actualisation are all impaled on the spikes of transience, decay and dissolution'. In his book *Happiness that Lasts*, he writes, 'I have said harsh things about conventional religion, but even more noxious is a dominant type of rationalism that finds no place for anything that cannot be proved by science'.

These words make clear that Martin would see nothing to be commended in the arrogant, dogmatic and much publicised atheism which has become a feature of western society. David Edwards, Fellow of All Souls, Oxford and Dean of Norwich, saw the future of religious faith as the gradual coming together of some elements of Christianity with Buddhism. Martin's belief seems to have been very similar. He writes, The principal use of religion is the practice of prayer and silence. The Buddha is the great world teacher; Christ is the great world exemplar. The hope for world religion lies in a mystical liberalism in which the enlightened mind is illuminated by that mystical love which is the very essence of God'.

Martin Israel was a successful doctor, a lecturer in pathology at the Royal College of Surgeons and co-author of a leading text book on pathology. He also became a priest in the Church of England with the pastoral care of a church in central London. He was a successful writer, a respected spiritual counsellor and a beloved friend to many. His busy, pressured and sacrificial life made constant demands on his time and energy but he saw every aspect of his work as sacramental – the outward and visible sign of an inner and spiritual grace; the grace of the Holy Spirit at work within him and through him.

When he writes about the absolute importance of the inner spiritual life he does so as a man of God and one of the prophets of our age. His teaching could not be more timely and essential.

Acknowledgements

The CFPSS would like to thank the following people who have contributed in some way to the writing of this Appreciation:-

Ivy Bishop, Patricia Borland, Margaret Bourne, John Braithwaite, Nikki Braithwaite, Tim Braithwaite, Noreen Breadmore, Revd Neil Broadbent, Barbara Brooks, Celia Burgan, Peggy Butcher, Linda Bywaters, Elizabeth Cane, Jeffrey Conrad, Rupert Cordle, David Cotton, Viscountess Marina Cowdray, Dr Kenneth Craddock, Revd Keith Denerley, James Donald-Atkin, Celia Douglass, Julian Drewett, Revd Dr Denis Duncan, Mary Fear, Gwyn Findlay, Max Findlay, John Franklin, Ingrid Fretwell, Dr Robert Gilbert, Revd Dick Hare, Revd Canon Dr Anthony Harvey, Helen Hazelwood, Dr Susan Heyner, John Hill, Linda Hinde, Jennifer Howard, Eunice Hughes, Dr Robert Jones, Mary Kelly, Cara Knott, Benita Kyle, Daphne Lee, Sister Margaret Mary SPB, Marilyn Mathew, Gwyn Morgan, Rt Revd Charles Mugleston, Stella Munby, Diana Myers, Norma Nowotny, Revd Canon Dr Michael Perry, Steve Press, Leslie Price, R. M. Sefton, Kyrin Singleton, Piers Skidmore, Beryl Statham, Meg Stewart, Jeremy Swayne, Davina Thomas, Jacky Thompson, Mary Thorne, Revd Kevin Tingay, Annette Tyler, Katherine Tyte, John Udal, Revd Hugh Valentine, Eleanor Vere Hodge, Revd Prebendary Francis Vere Hodge, Revd Nicholas Vesey, Laura Walker, Yvonne Walker, Dr Allan Walter, The Very Revd Alex Wedderspoon, Revd Peter Williams, Sheila Willson, Phillippa Winton.